W9-CGW-853

TEN STEPS TO FINANCIAL FREEDOM

Ten Steps TO FINANCIAL FREEDOM

For You, Your Family, and Your Country

Robert H. Schuller

and

Paul David Dunn

RUTLEDGE HILL PRESS

Nashville, Tennessee

Copyright © 1997 by Robert H. Schuller and Paul David Dunn

All rights reserved. Written permission must be secured from the publisher to use or reproduce any part of this book, except for brief quotations in critical reviews and articles.

Published in Nashville, Tennessee, by Rutledge Hill Press, 211 Seventh Avenue North, Nashville, Tennessee 37219.

Distributed in Canada by H. B. Fenn & Company, Ltd., 34 Nixon Road, Bolton, Ontario L7E 1W2.

Distributed in Australia by The Five Mile Press Pty. Ltd., 22 Summit Road, Noble Park, Victoria 3174.

Distributed in New Zealand by Tandem Press, 2 Rugby Road, Birkenhead, Auckland 10.

Distributed in the United Kingdom by Verulam Publishing, Ltd., 152a Park Street Lane, Park Street, St. Albans, Hertfordshire AL2 2AU.

Typography by E. T. Lowe, Nashville, Tennessee

Library of Congress Cataloging-in-Publication Data

Schuller, Robert Harold.

Ten steps to financial freedom : for you, your family, and your country / Robert H. Schuller and Paul David Dunn.

p. cm.

ISBN 1-55853-533-0

1. Finance, Personal. 2. Debt—United States. 3. Finance, Public—United States. 4. Debts, Public—United States. I. Dunn, Paul David. II. Title.

HG179.S324 1997 97-31485

CIP

Printed in the United States of America

1 2 3 4 5 6 7 8 9—00 99 98 97

Contents

Introduction
Robert H. Schuller

It was Monday, February 13, 1995. Abraham Lincoln's birthday was being celebrated this day because the twelfth fell on a Sunday. I was alone commemorating his birthday in his bedroom in the White House, sitting behind his desk, reading the Emancipation Proclamation written in his own hand. Lincoln's one bold commitment had set free four million Americans from slavery. America, not yet one hundred years old, did not have a problem. It simply had a decision that needed to be made. That decision would be painful. It would erupt into civil war. But the decision Lincoln made to set slaves free was the right decision. Abraham Lincoln did not surrender leadership to pressures that would promise painless peace at the price of immorality.

Now, at the invitation of President Bill Clinton, I was spending the afternoon behind Lincoln's desk. Later I would sleep in Lincoln's bed and in the morning have breakfast on the second floor of the White House. A few hours earlier, when I had walked with President Clinton to this historic bedroom, I had given him a copy of a book I had written with Paul Dunn ten years earlier, *The Power of Being Debt Free.* The president and I had prayer, and I watched him walk out of the door to go to his own bedroom down the hall. I prayed he would read the book. The next morning I stepped out of my door just as he came out of his bedroom. We met at the elevator. I was pleased to see him still carrying the book as he left to take *Air Force One* on an official engagement.

As I watched President Clinton leave, I wondered again—as I frequently did when Paul and I wrote the *The Power of Being Debt Free*—how many Americans are enslaved to financial debt and are unable to achieve their dreams because their first obligation is to payments on credit card balances or installment loans. I wondered how many presidents of the United States, because of our national debt, have lost their freedom to lay out creative, constructive, inspiring budgets—budgets that would build great cities, underwrite cures for deadly diseases, and inspire and motivate children to develop their potential. How many presidents in the future will be enslaved to a national debt that will demand so much money to pay the interest that neither the president nor Congress can dream great dreams for an incredibly beautiful, bold, and exciting future?

America needs another Abraham Lincoln! We need a leader who can dare to envision a great dream that will break the country free from the tyranny of this awesome, merciless federal debt. No person escapes the penalty of the debt. The debt keeps the poor from having the opportunity to discover—much less develop—their potential. The rich watch while a large portion of their taxes goes just to pay the $305 billion annual interest on the debt. No one escapes. We cannot vote on whether or not we would like to pay the interest; we do not have that freedom. Because of the debt, we do not have the freedom to choose where we want to channel our energies and our resources. Interest on the debt is not a choice. It is a demand.

Senators, representatives, and presidents all have surrendered their leadership to this profound force that heartlessly and greedily grasps the first money that comes to the federal government from the hard-working American citizens who—more than they know—have become the serfs to an economic despotism. We call out, hoping some visionary American will set the people of the United States free by announcing America's declaration of financial independence, just as Abraham Lincoln set free the slaves by announcing the Emancipation Proclamation.

The twentieth century has been a century of conflict: two world wars, the Korean conflict, Vietnam, and the Persian Gulf

War. But we have one last great war to fight—the war to eliminate the national debt and provide economic freedom for our children and grandchildren.

I'll never forget the evening I spent alone in Lincoln's bedroom. That night, before I went to sleep, I knelt at Lincoln's bed to pray. I prayed for my children. I prayed for my friends. I prayed for my family, and I named each of my seventeen grandchildren. I prayed for their future, for their faith, for their families, and for their friends.

It was also while I was in the Lincoln bedroom that I realized that although the book President Clinton took with him to read on *Air Force One* issued a warning America desperately needed to hear, it was written ten years too early. Not only has our national debt continued to grow—from $1.8 trillion in 1985 to $5.4 trillion in 1997—but the incidence of personal bankruptcy due to increasing individual debt has reached record levels. In 1985, Americans were not ready to do battle with the debt, the enemy that would do more damage to future generations than to us. But today I believe we are ready to fight the battle to achieve financial freedom for both ourselves and our country. Therefore, Paul Dunn and I revised our earlier book. We have brought the statistics up to date and added some current illustrations. We realized that we needed to offer ten ways to eliminate the national debt and also to spell out ten steps to eliminate debt from our families. Only by eliminating debt can we build a strong future for ourselves and our children, thereby announcing our declaration of financial independence.

I need to mention that when you encounter the pronoun "I" in this book, you can assume that it is Robert Schuller speaking. When you encounter the pronoun "we," you can assume it is the joint expression of the co-authors. Our ideas have mutually blended so much that it is frequently difficult, I must admit, to know what words came from which pen. The interfacing has been quite remarkable.

The goal of being debt free is possible—possible for you and for our country! And the power it can release for the future is awesome! If you are ready to think bigger than you have ever thought before—then read on!

Robert H. Schuller

Introduction
Paul David Dunn

Today America faces a crisis brought on by an excessive burden of debt—federal debt and personal debt. We are living on borrowed money. We are stealing from our children and borrowing massive amounts of money. A series of federal deficits has accumulated into an alarming federal debt. Our currency, once the backbone of the world's economy, now remains humbly weak against many other currencies, including the Japanese yen, the British pound, the German mark, and the Swiss franc.

The United States is still the leading economic, military, and philosophical power in the world. However, our weakness is our debt. Never before in history has a debtor nation led the world economically. In order for America's philosophical and political ideas to continue to have influence and value, they ultimately must rest on a solid economic foundation, for who would follow the lead of a country standing at the door of bankruptcy?

Bankruptcy? Not a nation as strong as the United States, you might say. But we are facing a debt so monumental that some claim it can never be repaid. The debt is so out of control that it is equal to nearly 75 percent of our gross domestic product.

Not only is America facing a debt crisis as a nation, but individuals as well are overburdened with debt. Consumer debt in the United States tops $5.2 trillion, including mortgages, with billions of dollars of interest paid out yearly by average working individuals. Personal debt, like the national debt, is not intrinsically bad—but excessive debt can cripple you and cripple our country.

There was a time in the late 1970s and early 1980s when being highly leveraged rewarded the savvy investor. Growth in the value of real estate rewarded the mortgage holder. The government helped pay for the cost of interest on consumer debt by making that interest tax deductible. Even inflation worked in favor of the person who paid the principal of his loan with inflated dollars.

Today, the situation has changed drastically. Consumer interest is no longer tax deductible. Economists predicted that this change in the tax code would reduce consumer borrowing. Once again, the economists were wrong. People kept borrowing. When inflation came to a screeching halt, those who thought it chic to be highly leveraged finally had to pay the piper.

Today, credit card debt is at an alarming level. Consumers have been preoccupied with shopping with plastic and their savings have dwindled. That means more and more families are working two or three jobs and will continue to do so for well into the future. Their inability to save for retirement perpetuates a nasty spiral. The spiral of increasing debt is one in which both we and our country are caught.

But there is good news. There is a way out! This book tells how to break out of the cycle of increasing debt. It also arms you with the skills needed to change your attitude toward your financial picture. Everything begins and ends with your ABC's—your attitudes, beliefs, and commitments. When you harness the ABCs of debt management, then you are on the road to financial independence. There are many rungs on the ladder of financial independence, but step by step you can make a difference for yourself, your family, and ultimately your country.

It is time to throw off the shackles of debt. You can do it. It takes an ordinary person who is willing to make an extraordinary effort to imagine the possibilities of debt-free living. But history is made by people who believe in a dream so intensely that they are willing to commit themselves totally to the realization of that dream. It is my sincere hope and prayer that you will share in this commitment.

Paul David Dunn

TEN STEPS TO FINANCIAL FREEDOM

One

The Power of Being Debt Free

Debt is the enemy of financial freedom. It's as simple as that.

This book reveals ten steps for you and ten steps for our country to achieve financial freedom. But these steps are all a means to accomplish one goal: get out of debt.

Academics tell us that debt is essential to economic growth. Economists proclaim that debt is not bad. In theory they may be right, but Lisa Perlin, chief deputy clerk at a U.S. Bankruptcy Court, points out that the driving force behind a current unprecedented rise in personal bankruptcies is consumer debt. "The ready access to credit is the reason that most people are filing [for bankruptcy]," she says. "It's hard to avoid credit these days." Both we as individuals and our national government have taken a useful tool—debt—and misused it to the point that it is no longer serving us; we are serving it. Debt is now controlling us. Whether we talk about our personal finances or about our nation's economy, our financial freedom and independence are being threatened by mounting debt.

This book will tell you how to achieve financial freedom. But the key is not the knowledge of what to do; we offer no new secrets. The key is the belief that debt-free living is possible and the determination to act on that belief.

There is a crisis looming in America. Our credit-based economy is being threatened by an unprecedented increase in personal bankruptcies and our federal budget continues to grow out of control due in large part to the increased interest payments on a $5.4 trillion national debt that keeps on escalating in spite of all the talk of a balanced budget.

But there is an answer. There is a way out of this crisis. Financial independence is possible.

■ ■ ■

The famous philosopher Sören Kierkegaard told the story of a flock of geese that prepared to fly from the cold regions of Norway to the warmer southern climates in their annual winter migration. After their first day's journey the geese settled in a farmer's field where they found a huge harvest of gathered corn. They quickly gobbled up their food, curled their necks to tuck their heads under their wings and, with full and satisfied stomachs, slept until morning. Awakened with the dawn, the geese stretched their long necks, looked into the crisp blue sky, and obeyed their instincts as they flew off to complete their migration.

But one goose could not resist the temptation to remain one more day to indulge in the extravagance of the food around him. He stayed behind, confident that he could catch up with the flock the next day. The second day the goose awoke with an even larger appetite, for his stomach was stretching from his daily indulgences. The more he ate, the more he wanted. He was hopelessly and helplessly addicted to what seemed to be an unending supply of miraculous wealth. Days stretched into weeks as the goose kept eating his fill of the farmer's food.

One morning, a cold and biting wind awakened the goose with a start. Rain fell from the thick gray clouds and quickly turned to ice at his feet. Alarmed by a revived instinct to survive, the goose stretched his neck, spread his wings, and began to waddle, then run as fast as he could. He had to leave today. Tomorrow would be too late. But why couldn't he run faster? Why did his legs move so slowly? Why were his wings so heavy? Why did his heavy body not lift to the wind?

Belatedly, the goose discovered his tragic fate. He had waited too long, indulged too recklessly, and ignored the call of his inner instinct too often. Now he suffered from the inevitable consequences of his pitiful procrastination. He could not take off because he was too fat to fly!

How serious is the economic situation facing you, your family, and your country? Have you been overindulging? The critical situation *is* very real because we Americans have been resisting or ignoring our instinctive call to self-sacrifice, self-denial, and self-discipline. We are facing the same fate as the fatted goose.

Increasingly the media and individuals are becoming painfully aware of an economic crisis that looms on the horizon due to mounting personal and national debt. An economic holocaust is certain if we, like the fattened, distracted goose, continue to procrastinate. We are creating a legacy of debt and financial bondage for ourselves, our children, and our country.

You and your family are probably being bombarded by solicitations to sign up for credit cards. The typical American carries five to seven credit cards with an average balance per card of $1,670. That's nearly $10,000 of credit card debt! The credit card companies encourage you to borrow more because they make so much money at it. Author and financial advisor Dave Ramsey calls this a "culturalized disease." The slick advertisements we receive promise financial freedom through increased debt. But debt is the enemy of financial freedom. This cannot be emphasized strongly enough. It is the central message of this book:

Debt is the enemy of financial freedom.

The idea that financial freedom can come through increased debt on a credit card or other means is a lie. How does debt of any kind prevent financial freedom?

- For yourself, debt makes all of your purchases more expensive and limits your buying power. *Forbes* magazine for instance, told of Paulette Mitchell who did not have $3,032 for a big-screen television she wanted and so she agreed to rent one with a purchase at the end of the rental period—for a total of $6,005.10—an effective annual interest rate of 55 percent. If she had saved for the television and paid cash instead, she could have purchased two such television sets—even before considering the interest she would have earned on her money and the better bargaining position she would have been in because of paying cash.

- Debt is thought to be essential to running a business. And yet every business person knows that debt means that the company must operate not in its own best interest, but in a way that pleases the bank or the lender. And the best interest of the bank and the best interest of the company are frequently not the same. However, John Crean ran Fleetwood Enterprises with a no-debt policy. "Any economist will tell you that you can't do that in our economy and grow," he explained. "All I can tell you is that it worked. In 1973, when the oil crisis hit America, the recreational vehicle industry was severely affected. Sales dropped off 75 percent. But because Fleetwood was a debt-free corporation, we survived while others didn't." John Crean experienced financial freedom.

- We have recently had severe battles in Congress and the executive branch of the government over the need to balance the federal budget. The battles have come over what to cut—whether it should be funding for the arts, for social services, or even the possibility of reducing the rate

> of increase of Social Security payments. A balanced budget could be achieved with none of these cuts if we did not have to pay more than $300 billion in interest payments on the national debt every year. Those interest payments have crippled our government's financial freedom.

The result of mounting individual debt is that personal bankruptcies in the U.S. have exploded, increasing 35 percent from 918,964 in 1995 to 1,242,700 in 1996. America is headed for a debt-induced bankruptcy crisis.

But why shouldn't we individuals increase our debt? Our federal government is doing the same thing by borrowing more and more. The following projections of what will happen if we do not reduce the government program deficit are frightening:

- Annual budget deficits of $100 billion or more will continue to add to the $5.4 trillion national debt;
- The federal debt will become truly unmanageable and create a financial crisis of unprecedented proportions;
- Interest on the debt will become unthinkable, even higher than the 16 percent of the budget that it currently consumes, especially if interest rates increase.

Financial freedom is possible for yourself, your family, and your country. The power of being debt free is a power of financial independence.

You can be a millionaire! You can enjoy the power of becoming a financially independent person if you make a decision to save wisely, invest smartly, and live with long-range goals. But to do this means investing and investing means you must exercise self-sacrifice, self-denial, and self-discipline. But if you do this, investing $2,000, for instance, each year in an IRA account that earns 13 percent interest, you will have $182,940 in 20 years, $351,700 in 25 years, $662,630 in 30 years, and $1,235,499 in 35 years. That $1,235,499 could earn more than $160,000 per year in interest. The truth is, you have the freedom to choose to become financially independent. You can enjoy the feeling of being debt free and knowing that you are giving that sort of heritage to your children. And what is true for you is true for our country. America can know the power of being debt free. But like the individual who invests in an IRA, the American government will have to make a decision to save wisely and live with long-range goals. We the people will have to support the government's decision to exercise some self-sacrifice, self-denial, and self-discipline. Only then will we have the power to promote peace, prosperity, and human pride worldwide.

Make no mistake about it. The road is not easy in the face of the seductive lure of easily borrowed money. For the individual that seduction is signing up for another credit card or buying an appliance on time. For the country that seduction is raising the debt limit. But additional debt only makes the shackles on our wrists and ankles tighter and the chains that bind us shorter. Increased debt restricts our freedom even more. Financial freedom is possible only through a change of attitude and habits.

We can solve our debt problems exactly the way we tackle and solve other problems: By getting down to the ABCs of mountain-moving, problem-solving, success generating possibility thinking. And what are these basics?

A—Attitude

Everything starts with an attitude. A negative attitude is certain to produce negative results. A positive attitude is certain to produce positive results.

Social philosopher George Herbert Mead suggested that attitude constitutes "the beginning of an act." He said,

> If one approaches a distant object, he approaches it with reference to what he is going to do when he arrives there. If one approaches a hammer, he is muscularly ready to seize the handle of the hammer. The latter stages of the act are present in the early stages . . . in the same sense that they serve to control and process itself.[1]

According to Mead, an attitude is not simply a point of view, a static state of mind. It is an integral part of action, a determinant of the course and outcome of any human act. Your attitude governs the way you act, the way the action will unfold, and the consequences of action. What can come about from a positive attitude is clearly exciting!

The financial crisis facing our country demands that we examine our personal attitudes toward our own debt and toward the government's debt because it is our money that is being spent.

B—Belief

Impossible situations change permanently when a positive attitude evolves into belief. Negative thinkers say, "I've got to see it before I believe it." The error in that attitude is obvious. The truth is, we've got to believe it before we see it. In every situation we have the freedom to choose what dreams we will believe in. Again and again the history of individuals, institutions, and nations proves the thesis that what we achieve depends on what we choose to believe.

1. George Herbert Mead, *Mind, self, and society*, vol. 1 (Chicago: University of Chicago Press, 1934), 11.

C—Commitment

Possibility thinking moves mountains when a positive attitude produces a positive belief that evolves into a concrete commitment. Again and again in sports, in politics, in war and peace, success does not necessarily go to the most talented or to the wealthiest, but to those who are the most committed. There are no great people. The difference between the so-called great persons and nations and those of lesser rank is a matter of commitment. Great people simply make commitments to greater goals. They dream nobler dreams. The greatest people in history are average people who have the commitment to tackle bigger problems than anyone else before them. The greatness of any generation will be molded and measured by the mountains it chooses to conquer.

D—Decisions

Possibility thinking works wonders because it is such a practical philosophy for creative decision making. In reality, problems are only decisions waiting to be made. I have counseled troubled persons with this honest evaluation: "You don't have a problem to solve; you simply have a decision to make!"

For more than forty-five years I have applied the principles of possibility thinking to every conceivable problem. Possibility thinkers are decisive leaders. Never do we surrender leadership to problems. We always let the positive, undeveloped possibilities call the shots. Never, then, do we let the problem-solving phase move into the decision-making phase. We make the right decisions simply because they are the right decisions, even if they appear to be impossible to carry out.

Again and again we see the miracle unfold. When the right decision is made in the face of impossible problems, the waters separate. Moses marches across the dry bottom of the Red Sea to the astonishment of the enemy behind him. The first step to living a debt-free life or to paying off the national debt is to make a decision.

■ ■ ■

We should be suspicious of any book that offers "ten steps" to solve *any* problem. Life is more complicated than that. But following the ten steps offered here for achieving personal financial freedom will start you down the road toward financial independence. Following these steps must be the result of a positive attitude that produces a positive belief and results in a concrete commitment and a determined decision. In the same way, if our country took the ten steps we offered here and coupled it with a change of attitude and discipline and determination, we would turn around the national debt and begin to pay it off so that our children would be able to enjoy the freedom and power that come with financial independence.

Two

Living Beyond Your Means—The Dangers of Escalating Personal Debt

In one form or another, debt reaches into the home of every person on earth, whether it is an international banker transferring money by satellite from Zurich, Switzerland, to Johannesburg, South Africa, or a nomadic Bedouin in the Sinai desert trading goat skins for the promise of water rights from an oasis.

Carefully managed debt is essential to trade and commerce. From the very basic level to the most sophisticated technological currency transactions, debt is a part of everyday life. Whenever there is a sale of goods and services to someone who agrees to pay for them in the future, debt is incurred. You incur debt, for instance, when you agree to pay your water bill after you have used the water.

When Debt Is OK

There are many times when it is moral, honorable, and smart to incur debt, both individually and institutionally. Few of us, for instance, have the ability to pay cash for our homes, and so we borrow the money and plan to pay the debt from future earnings. There are also times when we are forced by circumstances to incur debt, perhaps because of an accident or serious illness, loss of employment, loss of dual income through death or divorce, or other unexpected financial mishaps. But such times are not as frequent as we would like to believe because debt can easily begin to control us rather than our controlling it. Letting debt run out of control is what has led to the current explosion of personal bankruptcies.

Nearly forty million Americans have no health insurance, and many people who do have coverage often find that their policies do not provide adequate protection. A medical emergency can leave them with a debt of thousands of dollars in medical bills that they must pay themselves.

Losing one's job, regardless of the reason, can be a traumatic and sometimes terrifying experience. Corporate downsizing, plant closings, or business failures have put many people out of work. In most cases these people have been able to find other jobs quickly and go on with their lives with a minimum of inconvenience. Others, however, have not been so fortunate. It is estimated that nearly 70 percent of all Americans live from paycheck to paycheck with no adequate cushion of savings to carry them through tough financial times. That means that only 30 percent of us would not risk a debt crisis in the event of a job loss.

In recent years the number of American households relying on two adult wage earners has soared. While many spouses have chosen to enter the workplace in order to earn additional income to improve their family's standard of living, others have been forced to do so to ensure that their family will survive economically. When a spouse dies or can no longer work or leaves the household as the result of divorce, the financial consequences can be devastating.

While these uncontrollable factors can push us into debt, trying to "keep up with the Joneses" can also have the effect of increasing debt. And such spending is controllable. Buying the biggest and the best of everything just to prove to yourself that you are as good—or better—than those around you, even if you cannot realistically afford those items, leads to debt. Debt allows you to pretend to be something or somebody you are not. If you seek your identity in your possessions, the sad truth is that, while you may surround yourself with luxury, you will remain poor in spirit. And very often, as your possessions grow, so do your debts.

Not all debt is bad. But too many of us have let our debt run out of control. We not only borrow to purchase our homes, but many of us also borrow to purchase our cars, appliances, and college educations. Many businesses borrow money when they calculate that the cash flow derived from the sale of their goods and services can finance their debt and still return a profit.

Many prudent investors and speculators have borrowed money to invest in prime parcels of land and have seen the value of their investments increase. Others borrowed to buy gold when it was $35 an ounce. When gold skyrocketed to more than $800 an ounce, some investors received their investment back twenty times, more than enough to pay the interest on the borrowed money. However, this points up the danger of debt as well. Many investors borrowed money to buy gold when it was $800 an ounce, expecting its price to go even higher. When it declined to $400 an ounce, they were left not only with gold that was worth half what they paid for it but also with interest and principal to pay on the debt.

It makes sense to go in debt if you come across a once-in-a-lifetime opportunity. If you have a limited number of days, months, or years in which to take advantage of a passing opportunity and you have the cash flow to finance a mortgage, then you would be smart and responsible to incur a debt.

Managed properly, debt can be a positive means to growth and productivity. It's a wise course of action when it is used to buy something that increases in value or produces an income. But the debt most of us have incurred keeps us from financial freedom. Excessive debt and the resulting interest payments can be a strangling, crippling, restricting force. Debt can be draining not only financially but also emotionally. We set ourselves up for such danger when we borrow money to buy something that loses its value.

Borrowing Money to Burn

Easy credit has allowed us to become a nation of impulse buyers rather than wise shoppers. We buy what we want instead of what we need. We would rather have something now, even if we must go into debt to obtain it, than wait until we have saved enough money to buy that item outright. Consequently, we borrow to buy things that lose their value and all we have left is the debt. When you buy a house, the lender is supposed to make sure that the value of the house is more than the value of your mortgage so that if you are not able to make your payments, the house could be sold to pay back your mortgage. The same is true of a car loan. But when you buy clothes or theater tickets or a dinner by putting them on your credit card and do not pay the credit card bill in full, you have borrowed to buy things that have no value left after you have purchased them. If you borrow money to take a vacation, there is no collateral left when you return home—only the debt.

The principle that you should borrow only for things that hold their value was driven home to me by a banker when I tried to borrow money for something that literally would go up in smoke! In September 1950 I took my first job as pastor of a small church in Ivanhoe, Illinois. In addition to my $200-a-month salary, the church provided me with a parsonage. We had just moved in when I received a call from a church deacon. "Bob, I think you should order your coal."

"Coal?" I asked.

"Yes," he explained. "Your furnace in the parsonage is coal burning."

Then I remembered that I was responsible for all of my utilities. So I went to the local lumberyard where I was told I could order the coal. The manager greeted me enthusiastically and seemed to know exactly how much coal I needed: five tons at a total cost of $77.50.

"When can you deliver it?" I asked.

"Tomorrow afternoon, if that is okay."

"That sounds great!" I said as I turned around to leave, my order complete.

"Oh, Reverend!" the manager called after me. "That will be $77.50, please!"

I stopped in my tracks. I assumed he would bill me. "But I don't have any money with me. Can't you bill me? I'd like to open a charge account anyway."

The decision was written all over the manager's face even before he spoke. "Sorry, Reverend. But we don't deliver any coal unless it is paid for in advance." He went on to explain, "Your coal bin is in the basement, right? Well, if we deliver the coal and dump it in the basement, and you don't pay the bill, it's a heck of a job trying to haul it out. If you want a loan, you'll have to go to the bank."

Somewhat taken aback, I left the lumberyard and headed straight to the First National Bank. The manager greeted me warmly, saying he had heard good things about me. Finally, he leaned back in his chair and asked, "What can I do for you, Reverend?"

"I am here to borrow $75, sir," I said unashamedly.

"What do you want to borrow the money for? Whether I lend it to you or not depends on what you plan to do with it."

I knew I had an unbeatable cause. My needs were beyond debate. On top of that, I was a distinguished citizen of the community. Without any reservation, I announced my request. "I want to borrow the money to buy my winter supply of coal. I need five tons and the going rate is . . ."

"Wait a minute, Reverend!" he quickly interrupted. The smile was gone. A firm, tough business look replaced the sparkle in his eye. "Reverend, we never loan money to buy coal!" The words were spoken with final authority.

I couldn't believe what I was hearing. He must have read my perplexity because he went on to explain his position.

"You must understand something about banks. The money we have to loan is not our money. Hard-working people put their savings here. They trust us to use their money to make money for them. We cannot lose their money. Therefore, we can't lend money without collateral."

"Collateral?" I asked, totally ignorant. "What's that?"

"Collateral," he said with a smile, "is when you have something of value to offset the debt. If you borrow money for a house or a car and can't make the payments, we simply take the car or house and sell it. We pay ourselves back, and any surplus is yours. That's called your equity. But if you borrow money to buy coal, the coal cannot be collateral because you will burn it in the furnace. Then if you don't pay your bill, our customers will lose their savings. Their money will literally go up in smoke! My advice to you, Reverend, is run your personal and church business so that you never need to borrow money for coal."

The banker must have sensed my panic. "I will tell you what I will do," he said with a look of mercy. "If I loaned you $75, could you pay it back in five monthly payments of $15 each? There will be interest added on top of that, of course."

"Oh, yes!" I said with a sigh of relief. "I can make those payments. There's no problem there at all."

"Good. Then we have a deal," the banker said with a smile as he shuffled some papers in front of me to sign.

As I got ready to leave, check in hand, the banker stood to shake my hand. His eyes met mine. "Reverend," he said seriously, "remember, never again borrow money for coal."

I walked out of that bank with a $75 check and one of the most important economic lessons of my life. Never again would I borrow money for something that could not be held as collateral or that would not produce a product or service that would grow and appreciate in value.

Our Changing Attitudes

We Americans today do not look at debt the same way our grandparents did. They viewed debt as something bad, almost shameful. We, on the other hand, look to debt to solve our problems.

Consumer debt in the United States currently is estimated to be more than $1.2 trillion, not including mortgages, which represent another $4 trillion of debt. Consumer debt has more than tripled since 1980. The typical American household is burdened with more than $39,000 in debt, and that total is growing larger every day. How have we become so inundated by personal debt? For more than 150 years after our great nation was founded, Americans treated debt as something to be avoided except in dire circumstances. Most citizens saved their money and paid cash or bartered for the goods and services they required. They rarely incurred debts except to purchase a home or farmland, or to start a business. Americans were proud of their self-reliance, and on those occasions when they did go into debt, they felt a social and moral obligation to repay it as soon as possible. For my father and others, defaulting on a debt was almost unthinkable.

Work was tough in northwest Iowa in the early 1900s. As a teenager, my father, Anthony Schuller, could find only a job as a hired hand doing manual farm chores. But he managed to save a dollar here and there until finally he took a chance on his dream. With all the courage he could muster, my father stepped into the office of the local banker. Land prices in the area had been rising steadily. As far as Dad could see, the value of an Iowa farm could only go up. The bankers thought so, too. However, it was only a few short months before the Great Depression hit. Land prices plummeted. Dad looked back later and knew he "bought high," but he knew he could always draw from the soul of the earth to repay his mortgage.

Then the Dust Bowl years came. Suffering from the relentless drought, crops were wiped out. The raw produce Dad took to market was hardly enough to make the interest payments on his debt. He hoped and prayed for times to change, for miraculous record crops and all-time-high market prices for his eggs, milk, and hogs. Dad held on to his dream, knowing that in a few short years the payment of the principal on his mortgage would be due.

Then another disaster hit.

It was late one summer when I was home from college. The clouds grew dark as the noise of thunder rumbled in the distance. Suddenly, a long, balloon-like cloud seemed to stretch out into a twisting snake. It was unmistakably a tornado.

"We're going to have to make a run for it, and fast!" Dad shouted. We quickly climbed into the car and headed out of the path of the tornado. From several miles away we watched the twisting funnel make its path across our farm.

After it had gone, we headed back down the familiar country roads. As we crested a small hill, we couldn't see the top of the barn that usually landmarked our farm. All nine farm buildings were gone. There was no rubble, only clean white foundation lines where the buildings once stood. The pedigree breeding bull walked dazed in the deserted farmyard. Somehow he survived even though the barn was dropped in splintered pieces a mile downwind. All of the horses were dead. The pigs were dead. The machinery was gone. The crops were cut off at the roots. Besides the bull, only the milk cows survived since they grazed in pastures outside the direct path of the tornado.

My father's hand drew into a tight fist, and he beat the steering wheel and cried in agony to his wife. "It's all gone, Jennie. It's all gone!" The farm he nurtured, cultivated, and cared for all those years was sucked up in a matter of seconds. And the heavy mortgage he acquired years before would fall due in only three years. Everything he worked for was totally wiped out.

The insurance paid only $3,500. Sparing only a few hundred dollars, Dad took the money to the bank. "Sir," he said to the banker, "I want to make a payment on my mortgage. It falls due in three years, you know. I counted on a good crop this year, but now that is gone. But I want you to know that I plan to pay off my debt. I can't lose my farm."

The banker was visibly impressed, especially when my father mapped out how he planned to keep farming without buildings or machinery. With $50 of the insurance money, Dad bought a dilapidated four-story house. Piece by piece, nail by nail, board by board, we dismantled it and rebuilt our house. We even made a makeshift barn to protect the animals. The house was tiny and far less attractive than the one that was lost, but I'll never forget when my father said, "Well, at least the buildings are paid for!"

With renewed confidence the bankers extended my father's loan for another ten years. It was a moving moment when Dad came home that night and at the dinner table prayed, thanking God that he did not lose the farm.

I learned my first lesson about economics that summer. Debt is an oppressive burden when times are tough. And interest on a debt is the toughest and most thankless bill to pay.

Years later my father saved enough money so that he not only paid off his mortgage but also bought a small "luxury" house in the nearby town of Alton, Iowa. There he enjoyed the last years of life with the freedom that comes from being debt free. It is amazing how liberating that feeling was to my parents and is to those who experience it today. That freedom can be yours as well. Later we shall see how our lives would be different and our standard of living improved if we would discover the power of being debt free.

What has happened over the course of the last few decades to change our national mind-set? Why have so many Americans abandoned the long-held tradition of pay-as-you-go in favor of buy-now-pay-later? Certainly, advertising's messages of instant gratification have played a major role, but our federal government must also shoulder much of the blame. Since the late 1940s, deficit spending has been a hallmark of the federal government, particularly in recent years. During the 1980s, President Reagan ignited a deficit spending spree. Through massive tax cuts and foreign borrowing, the national debt increased from $907.7 billion in 1980 to more than $2.8 trillion by the end of the decade. In 1997 our national debt totals $5.4 trillion, nearly six times the 1980 level and almost double that of 1989. In his book *Will America Grow Up Before It Grows Old?* former Secretary of Commerce Peter Peterson states, "Reagan gave us a spectacular consumption boom . . . a borrow-and-spend administration, a feel-good decade in which we could have it all—without the bother of actually producing it."

Many Americans have taken to heart advertising's allure of instant gratification and the federal government's example of increasing debt. Millions now believe they can attain a comfortable lifestyle without making difficult spending choices, even if their finances take a turn for the worse. They feel they are entitled to a certain type of lifestyle and don't want to worry about paying for it until later. As a result there is an astonishing increase in personal bankruptcies of those who have increased debt beyond their ability to repay. They lose to bankruptcy the lifestyle they borrowed so heavily to achieve.

Pounded by Plastic

In the late 1940s, shoppers bought 40 percent of their department store purchases on store charge accounts. The amounts charged were usually small, and in most cases buyers paid off their debts in a few weeks or months. In 1949, Diners Club began issuing credit cards and many of the nation's banks followed suit less than a decade later. America's romance with credit—and debt—began to flower. The proliferation of credit cards provided a seemingly simple way for Americans to obtain for themselves a piece of the so-called "good life" that they saw on television.

By 1968, consumers owed nearly $2 billion in revolving credit charges, and within a decade that amount had skyrocketed to more than $53 billion. By 1984 revolving credit charges had continued to soar to about $106 billion, and by 1989, with the federal government leading by example, that amount doubled again to $212 billion. In the 1990s, declining credit card interest rates, lower unemployment, and more aggressive marketing by banks have pushed consumer debt even higher. Credit card debt nationwide has grown by 20 percent annually since 1994 and Americans are currently saddled with more than $300 billion in credit card debt. Estimates are that payments on credit card debt amount to more than 20 percent of the average household's after-tax income.

The Snowball Effect

One way in which debt enslaves us is its snowball effect. If your household income is $28,447, you probably pay about $11,113 in taxes. Your after-tax income is therefore $17,334. If you are average and have about $10,000 in unpaid credit card balances, you could be paying $1,200 to $1,800 per year in interest on that balance. If you are paying $1,600 in interest, that is

$1,600 you cannot use to buy other goods and services. Interest on this credit card debt alone is more than 9 percent of your after-tax income. You have effectively cut your income by $1,600. You could cut your spending by $1,600 per year, but too many of us solve the problem by borrowing $1,600 more to buy the things we want. That adds to your credit card debt and adds another $256 in interest the next year.

The only way to stop the snowball effect of increasing debt is to take drastic steps to reduce it. In the example of the average person, you should not just reduce your spending by $1,600, but perhaps by $2,600 or more to begin paying down the principal. The snowball effect then works *for* you instead of *against* you. As you pay down the principal amount you owe, the interest you have to pay also goes down, giving you the ability to pay even greater amounts of principal.

The Bankruptcy Boom

If the *average* credit card debt is more than 20 percent of after-tax income, there are many families that have debt that is much higher. Many people are buying far more on credit than they can reasonably afford to repay. Unlike previous generations, which "saved for a rainy day," Americans today have decreasing reserves on which to draw. Average household savings in the United States slipped to 3 to 5 percent of total income in the 1980s and currently averages a little more than 4.7 percent. The household savings rate in other leading industrial countries is markedly higher. In Japan, for instance, the rate is more than 18 percent. The average American family has less than $1,000 in the bank, which is particularly alarming since such a small amount would offer virtually no protection against a major financial or health crisis. The result of this increased debt is an impending debt-induced bankruptcy crisis.

■ ■ ■

The woman had not slept well for months. She was depressed and nervous. For nearly a year she had struggled to pay her bills on time but she just couldn't keep pace with the ever-higher monthly payments. No matter how hard she tried to make ends meet, there was never enough money to satisfy all of her creditors. Then the letters and phone calls from collection agents began, a few at first and then with increasing frequency. Initially, the collectors seemed to be understanding as she explained her financial plight and promised to try to bring her accounts up to date. But as time passed and the number of missed and late payments mounted, the calls and letters became more demanding.

Finally, as her worries mounted and her health began to deteriorate due to stress, the forty-two-year-old receptionist did something that more than one million Americans a year do: She sought relief from her creditors in U.S. Bankruptcy Court. Claiming assets of $80,000 and liabilities of nearly $92,000, the woman filed under Chapter 13 of the bankruptcy code, which will enable her to retain her house and car while devoting nearly all of her wages for the next five years to a court-approved repayment plan.

How did this woman get into such dire financial straits? "I got in over my head with credit cards. I loved that plastic! The companies kept sending me those cards and I used them. Before I knew what was happening, I owed a lot of money to a lot of people. And pretty soon there were more bills coming in than I had money to pay. At first, I tried juggling the payments to send money to the collection people who kept calling. But there just wasn't enough money coming in to pay everybody each month. Now that I've declared bankruptcy and have made arrangements to pay off my debts, I can at least sleep nights. And I won't have to worry about those collection people calling me every day."

■ ■ ■

Personal bankruptcy is booming in America. It often occurs when people sink so deeply into debt that they cannot pull themselves free. In 1996, bankruptcy filings in the United States increased by more than 35 percent from the previous year to a record 1,242,700, the first time that more than one million persons had filed for protection from creditors in a single year.

The driving force behind the sharp increase in bankruptcies, according to Judge George C. Paine II of the Middle Tennessee District of U.S. Bankruptcy Court, is consumer debt.[1] "The ready access to credit is the reason that most people are filing," Judge Paine said. "It's hard to avoid credit these days." He's right; Americans receive solicitations for credit cards almost daily because banks and others make *a lot* of money on plastic credit. In 1994, for instance, Sears, according to *Consumer Reports' Money Book*, made more money from credit cards than it did from the sale of merchandise.

Another factor in the rise in bankruptcy filings is that current bankruptcy laws make it relatively simple and inexpensive for people to abandon their obligation to repay debts. There are two primary kinds of bankruptcies: under a Chapter 7 bankruptcy a debtor's assets are sold to repay creditors; under a Chapter 13 bankruptcy a debtor's assets are protected from repossession while a court-appointed trustee devises a plan for the debts to be repaid. Many persons are using Chapter 7 bankruptcy to avoid repaying their creditors, even though with a bit of sacrifice and discipline, they could reorganize their finances and repay their creditors over a period of a few years. They are taking the easy way out and walking away from their responsibilities. A study published in 1996 by Purdue University's Credit Research Center revealed that 45 percent of people in Chapter 7 bankruptcy had the ability to repay one-third or more of their

1. "Strapped with debt, Tennesseans flock to file bankruptcy," *Nashville Banner*, June 4, 1997, sec. 3, 3.

unsecured debt over a three-year period. According to Visa U.S.A. Inc., bank cards lost $4.7 billion in 1995 due to personal bankruptcy filings—a staggering 45 percent increase from the previous year.

The increase in personal bankruptcy filings should be a cause of serious concern. You may not think you are in debt to such an extent that you are in danger of bankruptcy, but you are faced with constant seductive opportunities to increase your debt. Sometimes the only apparent way out is through bankruptcy. But just because we *can* walk away from our responsibilities through bankruptcy does not mean we *should.* Anytime we avoid repaying a debt that we have the wherewithal to pay, we are diminished because we have failed to follow through on a moral obligation. Instead, we must strive to repay all of our debts whenever possible.

Do you and your family want financial freedom? Do you want the independence, peace, power, and security that come from not having to worry about making the next payment on your car loan or credit card bill? Then make a decision now to take the steps given in this book to get out of debt. Debt is the enemy of financial freedom.

I have known hundreds of people who experience the peace and power that comes with financial freedom. They do not have to worry about bankruptcy or economic difficulties caused by an accident or serious illness, loss of a job, loss of a second income through death or divorce, or other unexpected financial mishaps. They are financially secure because they have little or no debt. This opportunity is not only for the rich. Any of us can reduce or eliminate our debt through the belief and determination of possibility thinking and by following the ten steps in chapter 5.

Three

A National Disgrace—The Dangers of an Escalating Federal Debt

Americans are facing a debt-induced bankruptcy crisis. The only way out of it is for us to learn to just say no to debt. Similarly our federal government carries an astonishing $5.4 trillion debt that will continue to grow not just until it balances the budget—which is still an elusive goal in Congress—but operates at a surplus. This growing federal debt cripples our country's ability to function effectively.

In the jungles of Java near Djakarta stands an archaeological wonder. Borobudur is one of the greatest monuments ever erected to Buddha. Built in the ninth century, it covers nearly ten acres, and three miles of bas-relief commemorating historic events in the life of Buddha cover its walls. When it was finished, Borobudur must have appeared to be stronger than the jungle, immune to decay. But as years passed and it was left unattended, the jungle began to encroach upon the edge of the monument. Beautiful green vines growing slowly upon the rock surfaces soon found soft spots and minuscule cracks in which to take their first hold. Surely, the vines must have looked attractive and harmless as they curled along the ridge of the monument. But soon, like a giant octopus, the vines overtook it. The quiet, slow-growing jungle overtook the seemingly indestructible temple. Years later, archaeologists cut the jungle back and began to rebuild the broken temple so that it could once again stand as an inspiration to all people.

Our national debt, like the jungle, just keeps growing. And unless the debt is eliminated, it will eventually engulf our society and strangle our economy. Every man, woman, and child, rich or poor, will pay a higher and higher price for the debt as it continues to grow. The national debt must be dealt with in the strongest and most responsible terms because it threatens to engulf our nation.

The intentions of our political leaders may be good, but we are deceiving ourselves if we think that a so-called balanced budget by the year 2002 will put our government on the path to fiscal stability. A balanced budget is not balanced unless it contains within itself a plan to begin paying the principal on the national debt. The time has come for the people of the United States of America to call for a declaration of financial independence! Let us unite to pay off the national debt and give our children the opportunity of enjoying the fruits of their labor and creativity.

Just How Serious Is Our Debt?

In spite of the recent budget agreement, which many expect to fall short of its goal of balancing the nation's budget by 2002, and modest efforts recently to curb government spending, the United States faces a tidal wave of debt that threatens to flood the economic fruits of the past two hundred twenty-one years. America's financial house is on the verge of collapsing inward. Our debt load is nearly three quarters of our gross domestic product (GDP). Interest of more than $300 billion on the debt consumes almost one fifth of our federal budget and is the fourth largest budget expenditure behind Social Security, social programs, and defense. Whereas other budget items provide needed services, interest on the debt produces nothing.

Even if our leaders were to balance the federal budget today—that is, eliminate all annual deficits—the size of our national debt would continue to grow due to the compounding interest on it. Estimates are that if the budget actually can be balanced by the year 2002, nearly $1 trillion more will be added to the current $5.4 trillion debt. If our nation does not put its financial house in order, America could face the fate of other countries that have failed to do so—hyperinflation, deflation, or a credit crisis in which the country defaults on its obligations, resulting in a currency collapse or some other catastrophic economic event.

The tidal wave confronting our country caused by the national debt is almost unbelievable, almost unthinkable, almost unmanageable, almost unsolvable. Here's why:

- Nearly $305 billion will be paid in interest alone on the national debt in 1997.

- The federal debt is so large that it represents nearly 75 percent of our annual GDP.

- For the ten years preceding 1995, our national debt grew by $1 billion each day. Due in part to the surging economy and increased tax revenues that sparked a significant decrease in the 1996 deficit, the debt is currently growing by an average of "only" $629 million per day. That breaks down to $26.2 million per hour, $436,806 per minute, or $7,280 per second.

- More than 40 percent of all personal income tax collected each year goes just to pay interest on the debt. That means your personal tax bill could have been 41 percent less if the government had controlled its credit spending.

- Taxpayers work until May 9 each year just to pay for their taxes.

- Government borrowing to finance the national debt consumes 70 percent of all credit activity in the U.S. Without such a huge demand, interest rates could be substantially lower.

- Over the past two decades, America went from being the largest creditor nation to the largest debtor nation in the world. Never in history has a debtor nation maintained its position of prominence and power among the world's nations.

- The personal savings rate in the U.S. is among the lowest of the industrialized nations in the world. Americans save 4.7 percent of their income compared with Germans, who save 15 percent, and Japanese, who save more than 18 percent.

An enlightening presentation by economist Dr. Gary Selnow on American Public Radio's *Marketplace* illustrated in graphic terms just what the 1993 national debt of $4.35 trillion cost Americans. Interest payments of $213 billion on the debt that year, said Dr. Selnow in the spring of 1994, could have been used to:

- Fund all the operations of the FBI, State Department, U.S. Information Agency, Small Business Administration, Federal Trade Commission, Interstate Commerce Commission, Federal Aviation Administration, Environmental Protection Agency, National Endowment for the Humanities;

- Fund the entire operating budgets of the legislature, the judiciary, and the executive office of the president;

- Pay half the annual salary of every man and woman in the armed forces;
- Pay the full salary of all civilian Defense Department workers;
- Train one million displaced workers;
- Educate a half-million students for two semesters at public colleges;
- Double federal contributions to victims of the Los Angeles earthquake and the great Midwestern floods;
- Build 150,000 quality homes for disaster victims and the homeless;
- Fund all highway construction, highway safety, mass transit, and railroad projects for the year;
- Cover all state spending for public libraries;
- Provide 350 research computers to libraries across the country;
- Purchase more than 7,000 hardback books for libraries in every county in the nation;
- Put 250,000 law enforcement officers on the streets;
- Pay the salaries of 250,000 counselors and caseworkers to help troubled youth and monitor released prisoners;

- Pay for all space flight control and data communication activities;

- Triple the government's contributions to the Corporation for Public Broadcasting;

- Pay for 435 postage stamps for each household in the U.S.

All of the items above could have been paid for by the $213 billion which was instead applied to interest payments. With interest on the debt in 1997 projected to be $305 billion—more than 30 percent higher than in 1993—it is easy to imagine just how much more our government could accomplish if it did not have to spend such a phenomenal amount to service the national debt. And America will continue to pay billions in interest every year as long as the government fails to eliminate the debt.

Deficit vs. Debt

It is important to clarify the distinction between the *deficit* and the *debt.* The *deficit* is the amount in a single year that the federal government spends more than it receives from taxes and other revenues. In fiscal year 1992, for instance, the United States government spent $290 billion more than it took in—a staggering increase from the $165 billion it spent more than it received in 1984. Public awareness about the extent and dangers of our national debt grew substantially during the 1992 elections, due in part to the relative success of third-party candidate Ross Perot's presidential campaign, which focused a spotlight on economic issues. A better-informed public pushed politicians to take steps to reduce the deficit and balance the federal budget. Those efforts, including a tax increase in 1993 that generated higher revenues for the government, coupled with a strong growth spurt in our nation's economy have resulted in smaller deficits in recent years. In 1993, the federal deficit was $255 billion; in 1994, $203 billion; in 1995, $164 billion; and in 1996, $107 billion, the smallest deficit since 1981. Although this is a dramatic improvement from 1992, our government is still spending billions of dollars more each year than it takes in. In 1996 it added $107 billion to the national debt.

The *debt* is the accumulation of all of the deficits in our country's history. In 1984, the Congressional Budget Office said that $114 billion, or approximately 14 percent of that year's entire federal budget, was paid in interest on the national debt of $1.8 trillion. By fiscal 1995, the debt had risen to more than $4.9 trillion and interest payments exceeded $260 billion, or 18 percent of the federal budget. According to the Department of the Treasury, at the end of fiscal 1996, with the debt at more than $5.2 trillion, interest payments totaled nearly $300 billion, or 19 percent of the federal budget. Projections are that by the end of fiscal 1997, the national debt—which is climbing at the astronomical rate of nearly $7,280 *per second*—will reach almost $5.5 trillion and interest payments will exceed $305 billion.

Much has been said about balancing the budget, which would eliminate the annual deficits. But balancing the budget is proving to be a monumental task because of interest payments on our huge *debt.* In the spring of 1997, a balanced budget amendment to the Constitution, which would have made it more difficult for the federal government to go deeper into debt, fell just short of receiving the required votes in the Senate, in effect shelving that important proposal for at least another year and probably the remainder of the 105th Congress. Instead, our representatives on Capitol Hill devised a bipartisan balanced budget agreement that proponents say will balance the budget by the year 2002.

Roger Brinner, executive director and chief U.S. economist for the consulting and information firm DRI/McGraw-Hill, spoke for many economic experts when he said, "Although balancing the budget is the goal of millions of Americans, the 1997-2002 budget agreement could pose problems in the future if our economy cools down and the government is unwilling to make tough decisions in the future."

How Did We Get Here?

How could our national debt have grown so large? How could it have gotten so out of control? In the course of our 221 years, we Americans have faced many crises that justified and necessitated borrowing money. In fact, many times we were forced to borrow funds because our freedom and the economic strength of our nation were at stake.

A child born in 1776, the year our great nation was founded, would witness in his lifetime two wars that would pull the country into debt. In the War of 1812, American soldiers went into battle while the new nation borrowed to finance their weaponry. Over the next twenty-three years the country completely paid off this debt, but by age eighty-four, that child would watch the young republic split apart in the ghastly Civil War. When the gut-wrenching battles were finished, the United States dug deeply into the pockets of its citizens to reconstruct itself so that in 1876, it could celebrate its first centennial birthday.

At slightly more than one hundred years old, America was hit with the depression of the 1890s. We recovered in time only to witness the greatest war the world had yet known: World War I. There were some who felt we should isolate ourselves from the conflict, but under the leadership of Woodrow Wilson, Americans decided to do their part. We wanted to make the world "safe for democracy," as President Wilson phrased it. And so, we again borrowed and prayed and believed that this was the war to end all wars. When peace was finally at hand, prosperity exploded. Great hopes and expectations allowed us to believe the bubble would never break.

But the bubble burst with a deafening noise during the Great Depression. Voices shouted forth, declaring that capitalism was dead. Masses became enthralled with the revolution that had occurred less than twenty-five years earlier in the Soviet Union, a revolution that promised economic equality to all. Franklin Delano Roosevelt courageously led our country out of this depression. The debt was increased again as people voted to borrow the money to create jobs and preserve our free enterprise system. It was during the Great Depression that federal entitlement programs—the largest and most familiar today being Social Security—were born. Although the majority of entitlement programs established in the past six decades have provided real financial relief to needy citizens, others have outlived their usefulness, have become grossly inefficient due to poor management and mountains of confusing regulations, or benefit only small special interest groups.

Prior to the depression, our debt was tied to the gold standard. But by an act of Congress in 1934, it was agreed that all printed money would be backed with the collateral of the people's deposits. No longer could we back up our paper currency with gold.

As the debt increased, America faced a second world war. We had been through the War of 1812, the Civil War, the Spanish-American War, and World War I. We couldn't afford another war! But Pearl Harbor gave us no choice. Our survival as a nation was at stake. With Hawaii still smoldering from Japan's surprise air raid, Americans were urged to take their money out of savings accounts and loan it to their country. War bonds promised to return 3 percent interest on the money that the government borrowed to buy the necessary defensive equipment and finance the military forces used to defeat the Axis powers.

With the unconditional surrender of the enemy, we continued to borrow billions of dollars to carry out the Marshall Plan, which encouraged us, as a noble and civilized country, not to abandon the defeated nations but to help rebuild them. We lent money to European countries and to Japan to launch their new economic and productive recoveries. Where did we get this money to rebuild these other nations? We borrowed it, of course, and in the process we increased our federal debt.

World War II was hardly over when we faced an expansionist international Communist threat. The Korean War engaged us, and then the Vietnam War drew upon our resources. After a defeat in Asia, our nation was in debt greater than anyone could have envisioned. Not only did we leave Southeast Asia with thousands of lost lives, but we pulled out with an enormous debt.

Our current $5.4 trillion debt is due not only to wars to preserve our own freedom and that of others but is due also to wars on poverty in our own country. We believe that the dignity of the individual is a nonnegotiable human value. Most Americans are willing to share their wealth to keep children and older people from starvation, to provide employment opportunities to all who are able to work, and to offer a high quality education to all young Americans.

In the early 1960s, John F. Kennedy started the Peace Corps to promote world peace and friendship. Peace Corps volunteers still share their technical knowledge with people in less developed nations. Later, Lyndon Johnson promoted the Great Society, a package of social programs that included Medicare, federal aid for primary and secondary school education, the Model Cities Act, the War on Poverty, and various consumer protection and anticrime programs.

America has come through a revolution, a civil war, and two world wars. We have enabled many nations to choose freely their own form of government. We have sought to provide economic equality for all our people. We have survived, but only by borrowing and therefore increasing our national debt.

We must make no apologies for this debt. Not to be in debt today would be at the expense of our conscience and our freedom. How honorable would our prosperity be if we did not share it with the less fortunate? How noble would our liberty be if we had turned our backs on the injustices of Hitler? How honorable would our freedom be if we had turned a deaf ear to the cry from weaker nations threatened by oppressive powers? Let us credit our past administrations for building up a debt that is essentially honorable. We gave our best sons and daughters and incurred an incredible debt to help other people who spoke different languages, lived in diverse cultures, and embraced religions alien to our own. The necessity and obligation of incurring our debt, however noble the intent may be, do not negate our responsibility to repay it.

The facts are real and frightening as we come to understand the enormous burden the federal debt and deficits place upon our economy. The thought of what might face our children is even more frightening. We have been called the richest country in the world, a world economic leader. But we must ask ourselves if we are really so rich. If we are that wealthy, it is only because we are spending the money that rightly belongs to our children, grandchildren, and great-grandchildren. In reality we are poor. Our national debt threatens to impose a taxation without representation on future generations. Concerned citizens, including you, can make a difference, and we will show you how.

The Entitlements Trap

Among the tough decisions our government must face if it is to get our country's financial house in order is the rising cost of entitlements. Americans from all income groups—not just the needy—benefit from entitlements, which are payments in the form of cash or tax subsidies made by the government directly to persons meeting specific eligibility criteria. More than 400 federal entitlement programs, including Social Security, Medicare, and Medicaid, consume more than half of our nation's annual budget. The 1997 budget agreement does not address Social Security, the government's largest entitlement program. But Congress will never be able to begin reducing the federal debt without reducing some of the entitlements.

According to the 1994 Bipartisan Commission on Tax Reform, outlays for just five entitlement programs—Social Security, Medicare, Medicaid, and federal civilian and military pensions—will exceed total federal revenues by 2030. That is bad news for the 76 million members of the baby boom generation, born between 1946 and 1964, many of whom will begin to retire during the first decade of the new millennium and expect to receive Social Security benefits.

The Social Security fund currently takes in more than it pays out in benefits, but this "surplus" exists only on paper, says the Concord Coalition, a bipartisan anti-deficit organization. Social Security is treated as an off-budget item. That is, it is not included in the annual budget computations. Thus, the paper surplus from Social Security is in effect added to the rest of the budget to make the deficit appear smaller than it actually is. Estimates are that by 2015, as fewer workers pay into the fund and more retirees file for benefits, the surplus will have to be used to pay those obligations in order to keep the Social Security system solvent. This has the potential to be a catastrophic problem because the "surplus" exists only on paper and would not be sufficient to cover obligations even if it were there in reality. When the "surplus" is used to pay benefits instead of being applied to deficit reduction, the deficit will increase dramatically. That in turn will add to the national debt, cause a dramatic increase in taxes, force major cuts in needed social programs and public services, and greatly reduce spending for defense and education. And that is just the tip of the iceberg.

Entitlements are considered "mandatory" or "automatic" spending programs, which has given many people on Capitol Hill and across the country the mistaken impression that they cannot be scaled down or eliminated. This is not the case; our elected officials *can* reduce funding for entitlements or even scrap the programs altogether.

The World's Largest Debtor

Most people think the national debt is financed by Americans. But the United States is indebted to foreign nations for more dollars than any other country in the world. Although the deficit has decreased from $165 billion to $107 billion in thirteen years, it is cause for alarm that the debt owned by foreigners has nearly tripled from $220 billion to $600 billion in the same period. This represents a significant shift in the economic framework of the world.

For decades, the United States was an economic superpower, lending money to countries in order to spur their economic growth. Now the situation has dramatically reversed. The United States continues to lend billions of dollars to foreign countries, but we are dependent upon foreign capital inflow simply to pay the interest on our debt. This saps money out of other countries' economies and makes the United States the largest debtor in the world. We have stolen from our children the legacy of a powerful, economically free country and given them in its place a country whose economic future may be controlled by others.

Because we need the money, we encourage foreign ownership of our country by promising to pay high rates of return to nations that invest their money to support our deficits. We offer high interest rates to attract their money with the hope that future production of our nation will be able to pay them back. To encourage investors, Congress passed a law in July of 1984 removing a long-standing 30 percent withholding tax on bonds owned by foreigners.

In an article in the *Los Angeles Times*, Robert M. Dunn, Jr., professor of international economics at George Washington University, pointed out the severity of this situation: "Advanced nations are supposed to contribute capital to the rest of the world. That is how we help developing countries grow. But the United States has turned this role upside down. We've become a net drain on the scarce capital resources of the world." In the same article, a chief lending officer of one of America's largest banks lending money to developing nations said, "If I were rating the United States as I do other countries, I would put it in the highest of high risk categories."[1]

▪ ▪ ▪

Our founding fathers warned us more than 200 years ago that there was no threat to our freedom greater than debt. Thomas Jefferson said it best:

> I place economy among the first and most important virtues and public debt as the greatest of dangers to be feared. . . . To preserve our independence, we must not let our rulers load us with public debt . . . we must make our choice between economy and liberty or confusion and servitude. . . .
>
> If we run into such debts, we must be taxed in our meat and drink, in our necessities and comforts, in our labor

1. Robert M. Dunn, Jr., "Deficit: Interest Threatens to Outpace Growth," *Los Angeles Times*, September 2, 1984, sec. 1, 7.

> and in our amusements. . . . If we can prevent the government from wasting the labor of the people, under the pretense of caring for them, they will be happy.[2]

Today babies are born throughout our country as citizens of the United States of America. They are our greatest national resource. The strength of our nation tomorrow depends to a large degree on the health and strength of our next generation. Consider what America's future would be if all babies were born with a genetic condition that would shorten their life span, limit their learning ability, and affect the development of their potential. If this condition perpetuated itself through the following generations, what would be the future of our country? The future of America depends on the health of the next generation. We can do something about it.

The increasing federal debt is an immoral debt. We have the right to borrow money, but only if we intend to repay it. When we borrow with no plan for repayment, we are stealing from our children. The federal debt is a crippling debt. It is more than 75 percent of our gross domestic product and the annual interest of $305 billion is the fourth largest budget expenditure. The federal debt is a growing debt. It has tripled to $5.4 trillion in a little more than ten years.

We can be a debt-free nation! To be debt free would give us real wealth and real power: power to maintain our middle class; power to wipe out poverty; power to educate all citizens; power to expand our human values worldwide. Underdeveloped countries could have their potential developed through low-interest loans and investments from America. No longer a debtor, our country would become a lender once more at low interest rates to struggling people worldwide. The money that now goes to pay off the interest on the debt of the past 200 years would

2. J. Peter Grace, *War on Waste* (New York: Macmillan, 1984), v.

instead spur economies around the world. Our children would know the power that comes with economic freedom.

As a nation, we have reached a time when we must grow up and face our responsibilities to pay off the federal debt. Then in 2026, when we celebrate our 250th anniversary, the writers of history will declare that the greatest battle ever fought in our first 250 years was not the War of 1812, the Civil War, World War I, or World War II. The greatest battle ever fought and won was the battle of the twenty-first century when the people of the United States of America waged an all-out war to eliminate the federal debt and liberate future generations!

Possibility Thinkers Lead the Way

In the two chapters following this one we will explain ten steps by which you can achieve financial freedom for yourself and your family and ten steps our country can take to reverse the potentially disastrous growing national debt. But we need to emphasize again that the key is not the knowledge of these steps and we offer no new secrets. The key is for you to believe that debt-free living is possible and determine to act on that belief. What makes the difference in your personal financial situation and to our federal debt is the application of possibility thinking. To some people reducing personal and national debt may seem to be an impossibility. But through the power of possibility thinking, impossibilities can be moved into the realm of the possible.

What precisely is possibility thinking? Possibility thinking is assuming that the ideal can become real. Possibility thinking is sifting carefully through all the alternatives and options, both real and fanciful, in the process of determining the grand objective that should be pursued.

The late Walter Burke, chairman of the board of McDonnell Douglas Corporation in Long Beach, California, experienced the challenge of possibility thinking when he received a telephone call from President Kennedy. As Mr. Burke described it to me, "The president said to me, 'Mr. Burke, I want to put a man on the moon. We both know that's impossible. Now let's figure out a way to make it possible. I'm calling you because we need to have a rocket with enough booster power to push a capsule away from the gravitational pull of the earth. I want you to tackle that part of the total project.' "

It was not much later that Walter Burke called me to ask if he could have a large photograph of the possibility thinker's creed. The same poster had been distributed to many locker rooms in professional athletic circles. We promptly sent the following poster to Mr. Burke, which he kept on the wall behind his desk.

WHEN FACED WITH A MOUNTAIN
I WILL NOT QUIT!
I WILL KEEP ON STRIVING
UNTIL I CLIMB OVER,
FIND A PASS THROUGH,
TUNNEL UNDERNEATH
OR SIMPLY STAY
AND TURN THE MOUNTAIN INTO A GOLD MINE,
WITH GOD'S HELP!

Possibility thinkers listen to every positive idea. They never reject an idea because there is something wrong with it, because it might create new tensions, or because it contains an inherent fault or negative factor, actual or implied, within the proposal. Possibility thinkers are smart enough to know there is something wrong with every good idea. Possibility thinkers clearly understand that all great ideas have imperfections. However, possibility thinkers believe that if there is some value or good in the proposal—no matter how preposterous or off the wall it may sound—then the proposal should be taken seriously.

It is not a mark of intelligence to scorn, scoff at, or snub some way-out idea if, in fact, it does hold some positive potential. History shows that great progress has been made by great dreamers whose ideas at the outset appeared unrealistic, if not ludicrous. Possibility thinkers explore with an imaginative and open mind all of the possibilities in a proposal. Possibility thinkers make an all-out commitment to discover hitherto unknown avenues by which an impossibility could, in time, become a new breakthrough. Strangely enough, this mental attitude alone has the power to release incredible forces that will move an impossible idea into the realm of the possible.

Pay off all of our personal debts as well as the entire federal debt? This gives us a fantastic example and opportunity for applied possibility thinking. The almost universal instinctive, intuitive, impulsive reaction is that this cannot be done, the task is far too difficult to accomplish. It has been observed that when a positive idea comes into the mind, we can almost always expect the positive idea to be immediately followed by a negative thought that can threaten to abort the positive idea at its conception. But every positive idea deserves a fair trial. Just because some splendid dream appears fanciful or unrealistic, if not impossible, no one has the right to rudely hiss the idea off center stage or rule it out of bounds. The greatest ideas always seem impossible when first conceived.

If they were well within the realm of possibility and general acceptance, they would not be ideas under discussion—they would be projects already begun. The greatest ideas are ones so embryonic that they are unborn and still waiting to be taken seriously.

There is a delightful story of the old fisherman who sat at the end of the pier with his line in the water. At his side was a bucket where he put his catch of the day. Next to the bucket was a stained and splintered ten-inch ruler. Next to the ruler was a can of worms. A passerby watched the fisherman's pole bend and saw him enthusiastically land his first fish. The fisherman carefully dislodged the hook, held the squirming fish in one hand, picked up the ruler, and checked the length of his catch. It measured just short of his ten-inch ruler. He seemed pleased and tossed the fish into the bucket. The fisherman soon hooked another fish, and the pole bent until the tip almost touched the water! As he landed this one, it was quickly obvious that it was far longer than the ten-inch ruler. The old man threw this fish back. The passerby was puzzled but said nothing. As he watched the fisherman, he observed that the little fish were put into the bucket to be taken home, but any fish larger than ten inches was thrown back. Curiosity got the better of him and he finally said to the fisherman, "I'm very curious. Why do you keep the little ones and throw the big ones back?"

"Well," the old fellow answered, "my frying pan is only ten inches wide."

We can laugh at this story, but in reality, every person is that fisherman. The truth is, we throw away the biggest ideas that come into our minds. We have our plans, perceptions, and prejudices, and if an idea comes along that exceeds or doesn't fit into our plans, we intuitively, instinctively, impulsively—but not necessarily intelligently—discard it.

The hardest job in the world is to think bigger than we have been thinking before. Thus, the ideas that are bigger than we are able to understand or embrace are offhandedly and irresponsibly discarded.

Intelligent and critical possibility thinkers have learned that ideas should never be thrown away simply because they are too big for our minds to grasp. We may reserve judgment. We may be cautious before we make a wholehearted commitment. We may quietly hesitate before we plunge ahead. But we discipline ourselves against the natural, normal, negative inclination to simply laugh the idea away and throw the big fish back into the water.

What is true for an individual or for an institution must be true for our country, too. We will all rise or fall, succeed or fail, move forward or backward depending on our willingness to master skills of good management. Management is the control of resources to maximize productivity. Success comes as we establish solid objectives and then manage our resources to achieve the determined goals that have been sensibly established. Individuals, institutions, and nations fail when they fail to manage. Some fail by mismanaging time, others by mismanaging money, and still others by mismanaging people. But ultimately, most fail when they mismanage the ideas that flow into their minds.

Possibility thinking is the philosophy that offers universal principles for the effective management of ideas. Ultimately, no person, company, organization, or nation suffers from a shortage of money, talent, or time. The problem is always an idea problem. Money flows to dynamic ideas. Talent is attracted to the corporation or the country that has excitement-producing ideas.

In the book *Tough Times Never Last, But Tough People Do!* I listed ten commandments of possibility thinking. These commandments can help us fulfill the dream of freeing ourselves and our nation from financial bondage caused by debt.

We believe this is an idea whose time has come. But how will this idea be received in the minds of people? How do we manage the thought? How do we respond and react to the proposal? Let us keep in mind the ten commandments for possibility thinking.

Commandment Number ONE

NEVER REJECT A POSSIBILITY BECAUSE YOU SEE SOMETHING WRONG WITH IT!

There is something wrong with every good idea. No proposal is perfect. There are flaws in every system. It is no mark of intelligence to find something wrong with a great idea. The question is, Is there something good in it? Possibility thinkers assume they can spot the positive and the negative elements in every idea and then proceed to divide the negative from the positive. The negative elements must be isolated and eliminated, or at least insulated or sublimated. Meanwhile, the positive elements in the proposal are extracted, welcomed, nurtured, developed, and exploited with adventure and ultimate success.

Commandment Number TWO

NEVER REJECT A POSSIBILITY BECAUSE YOU WON'T GET THE CREDIT!

We would plead with our fellow citizens that the proposal for achieving national financial freedom through the power of being debt free not become a political issue. A tragedy in a free society is the inclination of a cause to become a politicized issue. If Republicans are for it, then Democrats have to be against it. If Democrats advocate it, Republicans had better fight it.

When the bombs fell on Pearl Harbor, there was only one unanimous reaction: We must win the battle and save the country without concern about who gets the credit. The Republicans didn't stop to think, "Well, if we win the war, the Democratic president will get the credit."

Also, we are not the only ones to advocate a debt-free lifestyle. Author Dave Ramsey, for instance, says, "*Dump Debt.* That's right—do not borrow money. . . . Have a family meeting. Let each member participate in a plastic surgery party. That's right. Cut up your credit cards."[1] We don't care who gets the credit for explaining to you the wisdom of debt-free living. We just know that the way for you and your family to achieve financial freedom is to get out of debt.

1. Dave Ramsey, *Financial Peace* (Nashville: LAMPO, 1992, 1995), 80.

Great things will happen when a family, a company, a community, or a country pulls together to win a battle without any concern about who is going to be honored.

God can do tremendous things through the person who doesn't care who gets the credit.

Commandment Number THREE

NEVER REJECT AN IDEA BECAUSE IT IS IMPOSSIBLE!

Every great idea is impossible because what makes an idea great is that it is something that isn't being done . . . yet. And it isn't being done because it probably hasn't struck anyone as being a viable venture. I'm convinced that every time a great idea comes from God it is always impossible. The contribution that religion makes to society is the reminder that greatness comes when we walk in the arena of faith. And faith is making a decision before we can see our way through the whole pilgrimage.

Someone once said to me, "I will be glad to go along with the idea as soon as I can understand it." He elaborated, "I'm willing to become a believer once I get the answers to my questions."

I replied, "But faith is what you need when you can't get answers to the questions!"

Possibility thinkers don't reject an idea because it is impossible, because they can't get answers to their questions, or because they can't see how they are going to accomplish it. They welcome glorious impossibilities as exciting invitations to come up with a new invention, a new organization, or a new technique that could spell triumph anyway.

Commandment Number FOUR

NEVER REJECT A POSSIBILITY BECAUSE YOUR MIND IS ALREADY MADE UP!

Possibility thinkers recognize that ego, greed, and stubbornness are the three major causes of failure. They are the unholy trinity that block progress. Possibility thinkers do not want their own way; they want to do the right thing. "I'm not ego involved; I'm success oriented," I tell my friends and associates. After all, possibility thinking is pragmatic. I know that if I get my own way—if I'm wrong—I'm going to fail later. Then I can suffer a real ego blowout at high speed in heavy traffic!

So, possibility thinkers have the capacity to change their thinking drastically and sometimes swiftly. People who never change their minds are either perfect or stubborn. I don't know of an intelligent person who would claim to be perfect or who would want to be labeled stubborn. Therefore, we need never be embarrassed about changing our minds. Rather, it can be a sign of emotional maturity.

Commandment Number FIVE

NEVER REJECT AN IDEA BECAUSE IT IS ILLEGAL!

Under no circumstances should we permit or advocate or approve of an illegal act. But it is true that much progress is thwarted by regulations, ordinances, and procedures, as well as by county, state, and federal laws. The beautiful thing about a democracy is that we have the power to change laws. And the positive legislators are the persons who are constantly looking for progress-restricting obstacles that exist in society. Then, through legislation, they seek to remove these growth-stifling obstacles. We simply change the laws to allow positive possibilities the opportunity to come alive and bring greater opportunity for all.

Commandment Number SIX

NEVER REJECT AN IDEA BECAUSE YOU DON'T HAVE THE MONEY, THE MANPOWER, THE MUSCLE, OR THE MONTHS TO ACHIEVE IT!

The power of a dream outpaces the power of an obstruction. The weight of a positive idea tips the scale when balanced against the weight of the obstacles. In other words, a positive idea has the power to attract the kind of support that can compensate for lack of money, manpower, talent, or time. If a positive possibility is treated with respect and is carefully nurtured, it will succeed against overwhelming odds. Exciting possibilities have a magnetism that attracts the kind of support that can move them from fantasy to reality. Ideas attract money. Ideas attract talent. Ideas solve time problems, too. The important thing is the idea. Welcome it. Respect it. Trust it. Believe in it.

Commandment Number SEVEN

NEVER REJECT AN IDEA BECAUSE IT WILL CREATE CONFLICT!

Every new idea will stir some opposition. Every new proposal can offend someone. Every positive possibility has a price tag on it and not everyone will agree on the price. Every time we set a new goal we will incur some opposition. Every new commitment will produce a new set of conflicts. New tensions arise with every new move forward. Therefore, if we reject an idea because it will create conflict, we will never get anywhere.

Commandment Number EIGHT

NEVER REJECT AN IDEA BECAUSE IT IS NOT YOUR WAY OF DOING THINGS!

Ultimately, your way isn't important. The right way is the only thing that matters. Learn to accommodate. Prepare to compromise. Plan to adjust. A different style, a new policy, and a change in tradition are all opportunities to grow. Readjust your budget. Compromise your taste. Accommodate your lifestyle. You may have to decide that it's more important to succeed than it is to snobbishly adhere to your private preferences.

Commandment Number NINE

NEVER REJECT AN IDEA BECAUSE IT MIGHT FAIL!

Great success comes to the individual or the institution that has the freedom to fail. The *fear* of failure is the number one reason for failure, just as the possibility of success is the number one explanation for most human achievement. What would you attempt to do today if you knew you could not fail? What goals would you set for yourself if you knew you could succeed? What promises would you make if you knew you could keep them? What dreams would you embrace wholeheartedly if you knew they could come true? This is possibility thinking. It releases incredible energies, enthusiasms, and powers. Ideas that have great possibilities for failure are turned into astonishing accomplishments through the power of possibility thinking!

Commandment Number TEN

NEVER REJECT AN IDEA BECAUSE IT IS SURE TO SUCCEED!

Does this sound ridiculous? Not really. We have seen countless people reject positive ideas because they were afraid of success. "If I succeed, will people expect more from me?" "If I succeed, will I only set higher standards for myself that I'll have to live up to?" "If I succeed, will I be able to handle the success?"

Many companies are deliberately kept small and restrained from expansion by corporate chiefs who fear success. They assume, often correctly, that if the company succeeds, they will have to delegate power and authority to others. And to many founding individuals that is a threatening prospect. In the political realm, we all see reactionary politicians voting against great ideas that could possibly succeed and in the process accrue to the advantage of their political opponent.

■ ■ ■

The ten commandments of possibility thinking help us to manage ideas so effectively that we can be assured of success. Each one has told us what *not* to do. Now let's restate them in positive terms. Possibility thinkers are slow to vote no and naturally inclined to vote yes to positive ideas. The yes vote may be qualified: yes, if; yes, when; yes, but; yes, after. But it is always yes. The natural reaction of a possibility thinker is to vote yes to a positive idea.

Commandment Number ONE

SAY YES TO AN IDEA IF IT WILL HELP PEOPLE WHO ARE HURTING NOW OR IN THE FUTURE!

Possibility thinkers recognize that we are all stewards. We are entrusted with a life and are obligated to contribute to the welfare of the human family. Anytime someone comes up with a big, bold, beautiful idea, we do not ask, "Is it possible?" Rather we ask, "Who needs it? Would it help people who are hurting?" The secret of success is to find a need and fill it, find a hurt and heal it, find a problem and solve it, find a chasm and bridge it. If an idea would help people who are hurting, we have no right to vote against it. Our mental attitude must be yes. Perhaps yes, if. Maybe yes, when. Sometimes yes, but. Occasionally, yes, after. But never a total, obstinate, arbitrary, no!

Commandment Number TWO

SAY YES TO AN IDEA IF IT CHALLENGES AND MOTIVATES SELF-DISCIPLINE!

Every person and every institution understands the normal inclination for waste. Expendable resources can too easily be drained away through lack of self-control. Possibility thinking is interested in maximizing productivity. All of us must welcome ideas that, if embraced, would impose the pressures to work harder, save more, and increase the power base to give added strength to the institution, the organization, or the cause that perpetuates the nobler human values.

Commandment Number THREE

SAY YES TO AN IDEA IF IT HOLDS THE PROSPECT OF CONTRIBUTING TO PEACE, PROSPERITY, AND PRIDE IN THE HUMAN FAMILY!

In a world marred by poverty, wars, and humiliation in the human family, let there be no offhanded, impulsive rejection of sincere proposals that, however implausible and unrealistic they may seem, do hold some promise of moving the human family closer to prosperity that can eliminate poverty, peace that can eliminate war, and pride that can eliminate human shame.

Commandment Number FOUR

SAY YES TO AN IDEA IF IT WILL ENDOW THE GREAT DREAMS OF GREAT DREAMERS!

History teaches that there are dreamers, there are dreamers, and then there are dreamers! There are the dreamers who have a dream but never pull it off. There are the dreamers who make their dreams come true, only to have their dreams die out when they die. Then there are the dreamers who make their dreams come true and inspire their successors to perpetuate those dreams beyond their own lifetimes.

Any idea that will prolong the life span of a great dream of a great dreamer deserves to be taken seriously. There were those great dreamers who dreamed of colleges and watched their dreams come true, only to see those dreams die out for want of a perpetual endowment fund that could capitalize the dream through stormy seasons. The history of private colleges in the United States is littered with shipwrecked dreams of schools that were founded but were unable to survive the depressions, the wars, and other economic tough times. On the other hand, there are also colleges founded with the financial foundation that provided them an unbroken income, enabling them to survive the catastrophic economic earthquakes that history inevitably produces.

If an idea contributes to the endowment of a great dream of a great dreamer, listen to it carefully and take it seriously.

Commandment Number FIVE

SAY YES TO AN IDEA IF IT MAKES GOOD FINANCIAL SENSE!

I remember the first time I met W. Clement Stone. At the time he was reputed to be one of the wealthiest men in the United States. "What does it feel like to be super rich?" I asked. I'll never forget his answer.

"It gives me the feeling of power," he said. "It is a wonderful feeling, if you want to do a lot of good for a lot of people!" And he flashed his wonderful smile.

Great wealth gives you the power to do a lot of good for a lot of people! Any idea that holds the possibility of producing financial advantages for persons or institutions controlled by the nobler human values deserves to be taken seriously.

With its ideals of freedom, peace, and prosperity, our nation should strive to multiply its wealth. The goal of the United States of America should be to become a richer, wealthier nation so that future generations will be empowered to do greater good for the entire world. The poor cannot solve the poverty problem. The hungry cannot solve the famine problem. The enslaved cannot solve the problems of the oppressed. It makes sense for Americans to maximize the wealth that we have today and strive to become not only a debt-free nation but also a nation that will, like a great university, have its own endowment funds. A great president of a great college or university should set as prime objectives not only the establishment of the highest academic credentials but also the building up of an endowment fund to ensure that research and development can be carried out in future generations. That president should strive to build an endowment so that worthwhile students who lack the money to attend a university could be given an opportunity for a free education.

We should call upon America's presidents in the coming decades to understand that their role should be somewhat like that of the head of a great university. They should establish endowment funds and watch them grow. They should build endowment funds in which the capital cannot be touched but the annual earnings can be distributed. I have a dream of a day when the national radio and television networks will converge upon the nation's capital for the announcement of the winners of the scholarships given by the federal government to worthy students. Even as the president of the United States has handed out medals of honor to veterans of wars, and even as the king of Sweden has the joy of handing out Nobel Prizes to international achievers, so future presidents of the United States would have the joy of handing out prize scholarship awards from the endowment funds that have yet to be established.

Commandment Number SIX

SAY YES TO AN IDEA IF IT WILL BRING BEAUTY INTO THE WORLD!

Beauty is practical, too. Ideas that contribute to color and to cleanliness upgrade the quality of human living and deserve to be taken seriously because human beings are inclined to become more beautiful persons when they live in a more beautiful environment. Environmental ugliness contributes forcefully and forthrightly to moral decline and decadent behavior.

What will happen in American society if the streets are filled with potholes and never repaired, if the paint peels and is never repainted, if windows crack and are not replaced, and if weeds grow through the cracks in the sidewalks and are never removed? We can expect those conditions to exist and to spread like a malignancy throughout the land in the decades to come if our country becomes further financially bound by debt. We are one nation, after all. A debt-free America would be a wealthy America. And that would mean the power to ensure the perpetuity of beauty in our cities, in our streets, in our countrysides. We see beautiful parks. We see rolling hills. We see clean streets and clean cities. But it will be in direct proportion to the financial health of our land and its individual citizens.

Commandment Number SEVEN

SAY YES TO AN IDEA IF IT CONTRIBUTES TO A SENSE OF A CARING COMMUNITY!

If an idea has within itself the power or possibility of bringing divergent peoples together in a sense of brotherhood and sisterhood, it has enough value to be looked at honestly.

Many ideas are malicious in their intent. Some individuals and institutions thrive on being divisive. This is, after all, a natural, age-old, reactionary technique of insecure people who elevate themselves by demeaning their real or fanciful competitors.

The truth is that all human beings are living on the same planet, drinking the same water, and breathing the same air. Earth is a space vehicle traveling at the incredible speed of sixty-seven thousand miles per hour around the sun. And if planet Earth blows up, all nations will blow up together.

There is a beautiful teaching in the Bible that all people are created by God and accountable to Him. That makes us accountable to one another. The world is too dangerous a place today for any nation to be isolationist in its mentality. If one nation suffers, all of us will eventually feel the pain. If water penetrates a boat by entering the most insignificant room of the vessel, it will be only a matter of time before the captain in his luxurious quarters will be affected, too.

We must recognize the truth in the phrase that no man is an island. No nation can stand alone. We must constantly keep before us a vision of a world that is a united collection of human beings. And the universality of the human family's needs must transcend our individual selfish goals. If an idea will contribute to the possibility of happiness and health for all people, then it must be taken seriously, however grandiose it may appear.

We will not say no to any idea that holds the prospect of a world of brotherhood and sisterhood of human beings. We may qualify our response and say yes if, yes but, yes after, or yes when, but we will not say no. We have a dream of an America that is so financially powerful, a country with all its debts paid, a mature institution well endowed with cash surpluses, that it will have the power and clout to produce peace and prosperity for our whole world!

Commandment Number EIGHT

SAY YES TO AN IDEA IF IT WILL CONTRIBUTE TO THE COLLECTIVE SELF-ESTEEM OF A PERSON OR A NATION!

Self-esteem and possibility thinking are philosophical Siamese twins. The "I am" always determines the "I can." The individual or institution that has a strong self-image will dream noble dreams. The individual or institution that suffers from an inferiority complex will never dare to dream what it can do, what it can be, or what it can accomplish. More than anything else, an individual's self-image will contribute to the quality of the visions the mind creates.

Wealth and power, without genuine, healthy pride, are nothing. For more than a century now a new "science" called psychiatry has tried to arrive at an understanding of the ultimate motivation that makes a human being a person. Dr. Viktor Frankl, lecturing at Claremont Theological Seminary in Claremont, California, said that to Sigmund Freud the ultimate human motivation was the will to pleasure. Freud thought the single, strongest need within the human being was the need for pleasure drives to be fulfilled. Alfred Adler, said Frankl, thought the ultimate human motivation was not the will to pleasure but the will to power. Frankl himself, however, thought the ultimate human motivation was the will to meaning. He said that more than anything else, people need to see that there is some meaning, some value, some purpose to what is going on.

I thought about that lecture for many years. It directed me down avenues of study in books and in conferences. Years later in a three-hour private dialogue with the esteemed Dr. Frankl, I shared my position: "Dr. Frankl, I submit that deeper than the will to pleasure, deeper than the will to power, deeper than the will to meaning is the *will to dignity.*"

Even meaning loses meaning unless and until it feeds my need for self-esteem and human dignity. We now know from behavioral sciences that the lack of self-esteem is the single most important cause of almost every negative human behavior imaginable. Any idea, therefore, that contributes to a personal or collective sense of self-esteem ought to seriously attract our support.

The goal of freedom from debt as individuals and as a nation holds the prospect of building confident individuals and a country that will enjoy a patriotic self-esteem at the highest level of any nation in the history of the human race. Psychologists have long known that people with a strong sense of self-esteem tend to be open, generous, and nondefensive. Therefore, they are easy and wonderful to live with. That's the kind of America that the world would welcome! On the other hand, insecure people and insecure nations, suffering from inferiority complexes or a lack of noble pride, are defensive, selfish, and basically dangerous.

Commandment Number NINE

SAY YES TO AN IDEA IF IT IS A POSITIVE SOLUTION TO A NEGATIVE CONDITION!

Possibility thinkers are aware of the fact that there is a positive and a negative solution to every problem.

The challenge of morality is to accept the restraints of law that would protect us from the temptation to select the negative solutions to human problems. For instance, the Ten Commandments in the Old Testament given by God to Moses were not designed to keep human beings from enjoying life. They were given to protect us from the negative solutions to human pressures and problems. Reckless antisocial behavior will ultimately rob us of the joy of living. For instance, people who kill can expect to be killed. Men who commit adultery can expect to fight with the husband of a philandering wife. People who lie can expect to lose the confidence and trust of fellow human beings. Moral restraints protect us from the inclination to accept negative solutions to problems. To get out of a problem by lying is the negative approach. We welcome, then, solutions to problems that are within the restraints of moral law and that would protect us from taking the cheap and easy way out of a predicament.

The vast majority of religious people have always opposed abortion, because they view abortion as a negative solution to a problem. The positive solution would be to allow a unique creature, a one-of-a-kind individual, to come into human existence and have his or her chance to contribute to society. Ideas that restrict our moral freedoms are not to be viewed as violations of our liberty but are to be seen primarily as screens that can protect us from the temptation to accept negative solutions.

The elimination of our personal and national debts is a moral issue. To continue to increase debt for our personal self-indulgences today is endangering the financial security of our family. To pass on the expense of servicing our national debt to unborn generations is a form of taxation without representation. It is actually theft!

Commandment Number TEN

SAY YES TO AN IDEA IF IT CHALLENGES US TO THINK BIGGER AND HAVE MORE FAITH!

Any idea that would help the human family and at the same time would appear to be impossible is to be welcomed as a challenge to our belief system. In 1967, the World Psychiatric Congress was held in Madrid, Spain. The closing session dealt with "Human Values of Psychotherapy." The first lecturer dealt with the human value of faith. The second lecturer dealt with the human value of hope. The third lecturer dealt with the human value of love. More than four thousand delegates at the convention, including me, heard the challenge to welcome opportunities that would build faith, inspire hope, or generate love. These qualities mark emotionally and mentally healthy persons.

The same can apply to a nation. How can we build faith? Any great idea that appears to be impossible holds the fabulous potential of becoming a faith-building experience. Individuals and institutions are only as strong as their inner confidence and belief systems. Ultimately, this inner spirit of dynamic faith cannot be inherited, nor can it be institutionalized effectively in a Declaration of Independence, a Bill of Rights, or a national Constitution. Ultimately, it must be discovered by each new generation. Each new generation must face its own mountain and move it! Each new generation must confront its own wars and win them! Each new generation must tackle its own impossible challenge and overcome it! This continuous process of discovery, rediscovery, and renewal of belief and faith is made possible as new ideas come to challenge us to move some glorious impossibility into the realm of the possible.

Creativity Solves Problems

We Americans have a history of producing innovative solutions to unsolvable problems, of creating new ideas for new tomorrows. In the 1940s, scientists were certain that an airplane could not travel faster than the speed of sound. But a group of United States Air Force pilots believed it was possible, and in 1947, Captain Charles Yeager broke the sound barrier. Since then, airplanes have traveled in excess of five times the speed of sound.

In a Los Angeles ear clinic, deaf children and adults are being made to hear for the first time in their lives. Through an ingenious electronic implant in the inner ear, microscopic hair follicles are stimulated to transfer the vibrations of sound into nerve impulses, successfully restoring the sensation of sound to hundreds of hearing-impaired people.

In the Midwest, the lithotripter, a kidney stone crusher, was developed to treat patients with shock waves in order to dissolve kidney stones without the usual painful surgery and prolonged recovery time.

In all fields of life, human beings have solved unsolvable problems or created new and innovative methods of dealing with their problems. The imagination of the human being constantly amazes us with the wonderful products and services being created.

If we can break the sound barrier, make people who are deaf hear, and develop machines and medicines to heal our hurts, isn't it possible that we can creatively fulfill the goal of debt-free living for ourselves and our nation? Or is that too idealistic? Who will really make the world a better place, the realist or the idealist? The cynic or the dreamer? It is the dreamer who becomes the uplifting force that gives people and institutions a vision. Without dreams and visions, we will die!

The Man of La Mancha is a musical play based on the Spanish classic *Don Quixote.* The dreamer Don Quixote sees windmills as evil knights, his decrepit horse as a noble steed, and an ugly cleaning lady in an inn, who is also an abused prostitute, as a beautiful and high-bred maiden. The beautiful part of the story is that those who listen to him become more like Don Quixote's dreams. He gives them self-esteem.

When confronted by cold, calculating cynics for being a wild dreamer, Don Quixote responds, "Who's crazy? Am I crazy because I see the world as it could become? Or is the world crazy because it sees itself as it is?"

The dream of a debt-free society through possibility thinking is the hope our future generations have for a fiscally stable society. Unless as a nation we are motivated to believe that our economic freedom is possible, then we will give in to the crippling forces of our rising debt.

The solution does not lie in intricate details of economic theory. The key is not found by fine tuning government policies. The key is to be found in two words: *attitude* and *commitment.* We need a positive attitude that arises from a firm belief that we *can* succeed, and we need a strong commitment to accomplish the goal, no matter what the cost. That commitment should be the result of a careful decision. If we have an open, creative, positive attitude as we seek ways to pay off our debts and if we make a solid commitment to pay it off before we know how to solve all of the problems, then we will have taken the most important step.

Attitude

Consider the difference an attitude makes within a financially troubled company. Two corporate giants—the Manville Corporation and Chrysler Corporation—both faced financial problems that would make even the most optimistic financial consultant cringe. One company chose bankruptcy; the other has risen to reclaim its rightful place among the leading corporations of America. What made the difference? It wasn't the rescue loans. It wasn't the quality of the product. It wasn't the cooperation of the unions. All of those factors were important to Chrysler, but the real difference was a positive attitude.

In August 1982, the directors of the Manville Corporation sat around their boardroom table discussing their corporate problems and bleak future. The billion-dollar forest products and construction company was faced with 16,500 lawsuits as a result of its role in producing asbestos-related products. Although the corporation was financially sound and had a low debt-to-equity ratio, it filed for bankruptcy because of the potential loss from the lawsuits. The directors had decided their problems were unsolvable. Why should they drag out the inevitable? Why not just declare bankruptcy? Throw in the towel. Let's quit!

The *Wall Street Journal* reported that the move was "highly unusual and unexpected."[2] The stockholders' equity plummeted from a high of $26.50 per share to nothing. The corporate leaders had lost control, and the company and all the investors had lost their money and faith.

In another part of America several years earlier, the directors of the Chrysler Corporation met to discuss their financial problems. The country was in a deep recession. Auto sales had fallen off dramatically and the company was billions of dollars in debt. In 1980, it lost $1.7 billion, the largest operating loss in United States corporate history. The future looked bleak. If any company should give up, it should have been Chrysler. But after hours of deliberation, a decision was made: We will not quit! There will be a way. We don't know what it is, but we will find it. We are willing to make changes. We are willing to listen.

Over the next six months, the unions agreed to unprecedented "givebacks." Twenty thousand white-collar jobs were eliminated as overhead was cut. The federal government made loan guarantees of $1.2 billion (on which it has earned an estimated $800 million in interest and fees). The engineers designed new and better products. The number of different parts needed fell from fifty-three thousand in 1981 to fewer than forty thousand in 1984. Chrysler's directors had a positive attitude that

2. "Manville's Big Concern As It Files in Chapter 11 is Litigation, Not Debt," *Wall Street Journal*, August 27, 1982, 1, 8.

arose from a firm belief that they would succeed in their goal of putting their corporation back on its feet as a leading automaker in America.

By August 1982—the same month Manville declared bankruptcy—Chrysler had paid off all of its government-backed debts. It reemployed and offered job security to thousands of union members. It designed a new and exciting line of products, including minivans and the reborn convertible! Chrysler stock soared from $2 to $36 a share. Its investors made money and gained renewed confidence in the company. Its challenging slogan became known nationwide: If you can find a better built car, buy it! Chrysler's corporate chief, Lee Iacocca, was acclaimed by several polls as one of the most respected corporate leaders in America.

What was the difference between Chrysler's success and Manville's bankruptcy? Attitude! There were many important factors along Chrysler's comeback road, but the most important element, the impulse that pushed the company to the top, was the decision not to quit but to win and succeed. The directors realized they didn't have a money problem; they just had an idea problem.

The effect of the attitude factor goes beyond the financial boardrooms of America. It can also make the difference in whether we as individuals and as a nation survive as sound financial entities.

Commitment

A positive attitude that arises from a firm belief that one can succeed is essential. But action is also necessary. There needs to be a strong commitment to accomplish a goal, no matter what the cost.

The famous scientist René DuBos once said in effect that the human being has a natural and overwhelming inclination to adjust downward. It was one of the reasons why he could be tempted to be a cynic and pessimist.

Adjustment is always a downward movement. Upward movement is never an adjustment; it is always a commitment. Any person, company, or country that has faced financial disaster and pulled out of it did so because of a commitment.

Not to make a commitment is to commit to do nothing. Without a commitment, the natural adjustment downward will begin to take control. It is time for the American people to stop accepting the downward pressures that could lead to financial ruin. We need to make a commitment to move forward and upward again to become more financially secure.

I personally experienced this commitment-making process and the outcome when our church was in the process of building our new sanctuary, the Crystal Cathedral. Architect Philip Johnson delivered a six-inch plastic model of what is today an all-glass church 414 feet long and 126 feet high. I took one look at it and said, "Wow! That has to be built! How much will it cost?" Philip Johnson answered, "About $7 million."

I quickly calculated in my mind what that would cost if it were mortgaged at the then-current interest rate. To borrow $7 million at 9 percent interest, our annual interest payment would be approximately $630,000 the first year! And our total church income was only $2 million. I could not envision how we could have a capital funds drive that would bring in an additional $630,000 a year. We simply did not have that kind of financial base.

The project was financially impossible. But I could not accept the word impossible. I also could not think of borrowing that much money and increasing our indebtedness. It was a totally impossible dream from a financial perspective, unless I could make a radical, revolutionary, 180-degree turn in my thinking, namely, to pay cash and dedicate the building debt free. But that brought out a contradiction: If we couldn't make a $630,000 annual payment, how could we possibly raise $7 million?

Desperate, I decided to play the possibility thinking game. I started to write down ten ways to do what I knew was impossible. When you do this, you will be surprised how your attitude will change from "it's impossible" to "it might be possible." I wrote down ways we could pay cash for the building:

1. Find 1 person who could donate $7,000,000. (That was good for a laugh, which at least relaxed me to keep going.)
2. Find 7 people who could donate $1,000,000 each.
3. Find 14 people who could donate $500,000 each.
4. Find 28 people who could donate $250,000 each.
5. Find 70 people who could donate $100,000 each.
6. Find 100 people who could donate $70,000 each.
7. Find 140 people who could donate $50,000 each.
8. Find 280 people who could donate $25,000 each.
9. Sell all 10,866 windows in the Cathedral for $500 each. (That would raise more than $5 million.)

That was as far as I got. I was already enthusiastic. I believed that the project was possible when only minutes before I believed it was a total impossibility. Creativity happens when you are released from anxieties and tensions. As I relaxed and had fun dreaming up ways to pay for the cathedral, I was able to break out of my negative-thinking predicament.

I knew I had to get one $1 million kickoff gift to lead the enthusiasm for this project. But I didn't know anyone that rich. I remembered reading about a local businessman who had given a $1 million gift to the YMCA. I didn't know him, but I contacted him. When I arrived at his home and showed him the model of the Crystal Cathedral, he whistled with excitement.

"What will you need to get it going?" he asked.

"A leadoff gift of $1 million. That would show everyone that this is something big that is going to happen. Then people will take it seriously. I'd like you to give that $1 million."

Suddenly, he lost his enthusiasm. "Well," he stammered, "I would like to, but I can't."

"Okay," I said. "I'd like to close our visit with prayer." And with that I prayed, "Thank You, God, that John wants to give $1 million. But he says he can't. Please make it possible for him to give it."

I left his house never expecting to see him again. The next morning I received a phone call from him. "Reverend," he said, "it is not a question of *if*. It is a question of *how* and *when*."

I almost fainted with ecstasy. He continued, "That building has to be built. I'll give you a million dollars, but I cannot tell you how or when I'll give it."

Within sixty days he delivered fifty-five thousand shares of his company's stock valued at more than $18 a share. Suddenly, the $7 million building looked feasible. But then we decided to build a complete basement, which immediately increased the cost by 50 percent. So we launched a donation campaign to "sell" 10,866 windows at $500 each. The response was fantastic. It looked as if we could pay cash for the building after all.

Then the unexpected happened. Double-digit inflation hit the marketplace. In just twelve months our project was no longer costing $10 million but $13 million. One year later, when we were twenty-four months into planning the program, the cost had increased by another $3 million. We were up to $16 million. Suddenly, before we knew it, the cathedral was going to cost $20 million!

What could we do? I knew what I would do. I took a break. I was on vacation when the church board met to consider an unexpected commercial loan offer for $10 million. It would allow us to proceed without the enormous strain of fundraising. I returned home to find that the board had accepted the loan.

I was not enthusiastic. How could we pay the interest on $10 million? And the loan was to be tied to the prime rate! Neither I nor a single member of that church board could foresee that by the time the cathedral was completed, the prime rate would be 20 percent!

All I knew was that once we accepted the loan, the pressure would be off my back to try to solicit major gifts from people I hadn't even met yet. Getting a loan has a way of making a person feel as if the job is done! In fact, it is only a big show. You've only deferred the payment.

I was still consumed by my grandest dream: pay for the building and dedicate it debt free. Then when the dedication ceremony was over, I wouldn't be left with the horrendous job of balancing the budget year after year. I made a personal decision not to finish the building unless it could be totally underwritten by cash gifts or cash pledges.

It meant crisscrossing the country building new friendships, selling the cathedral idea, and soliciting funds to get it built. I kept remembering the saying, "Whatever the mind can conceive, the human being can achieve."

On September 18, 1980, the Crystal Cathedral opened its doors. It was an international press event noted and photographed in major media publications around the world. But the only thing that impressed me was that God had answered our prayers.

The cost topped $20 million. We had collected just under $17 million. Almost $4 million had been pledged to be given over the next thirty-six months. That was covered by a 9 percent fixed-rate mortgage by our local bank. We announced that the building was dedicated debt free, and in fact, all of the pledges were made good in the next three years.

I felt free! Feelings of "isn't it great not to have a debt" flooded over me. I thought, *Isn't it wonderful not to have to take money out of the offering plate to pay the interest on the mortgage? All the money can go to programs that meet human needs here and now.*

There is nothing like the power of being debt free. It is time for us as private citizens and as a nation to experience that feeling. We can experience this power. It all starts with an attitude. Then it takes a commitment. If we make a total commitment to pay off our personal debts as well as our national debt, it will be possible to do it.

There is no hopeless situation until we become a hopeless people. Great ideas to solve our personal and national debt crises will come from ordinary people, for great people are ordinary people with an extraordinary amount of determination.

Five

Ten Ways to Accomplish the Impossible— For You and Your Family

As I began to write this, I was interrupted by a ringing telephone. Rather than let the machine screen the call, I answered the phone. A saleswoman immediately congratulated me. I had been selected—singled out—to receive a new platinum credit card. I should feel privileged.

I listened politely until I could courteously decline the special offer. As I hung up and returned to my yellow pad, I smiled at the irony. I'm writing to encourage others to find financial freedom, and I am bombarded with offers for credit that I don't want or need. Free airline tickets, free clocks, and free perks are used to entice me to sign up for more debt. But as the old adage says, If it looks too good to be true, it is!

Personal debt, like our national debt, is not intrinsically evil or wrong. Personal debt, managed properly, can help you to buy financial assets like a home, which otherwise would be out of reach for most people. However, unbridled and undisciplined credit is a vicious cycle that can destroy the greatest of personal dreams. James Grant, editor of *Grant's Interest Rate Observer*, put it wisely. "Debt is a kind of household tool; it's like a rope. You can use it for lifting or many other helpful tasks, or you can use it to hang yourself."

Our goal in this chapter is to help you regain control of your dreams and provide the knowledge and skills needed to bring them to reality. Financial freedom, like any great goal, is not achieved without paying the price. In this case, we mean literally *paying the price*! Join us now as we begin a journey of ten steps to your own personal financial freedom.

Step One: Recognize Your Responsibility

"If it's going to be, it's up to me."

Your financial freedom—or lack of it—is due in full to the decisions *you* make. Perhaps the most important lesson you can learn from this book is contained in this sentence: "If it's going to be, it's up to me." No one has greater power to control the financial destiny of your future than you. Even if you were miraculously given one million dollars, your success or failure would still be determined by you. I am here to tell you that you can achieve financial freedom no matter who you are or where you stand on the financial ladder. When you hold the conviction that success comes from within, then you will be standing on solid ground to begin an incredible journey.

Excessive spending, divorce, medical emergencies, business failures—all devastating problems—might tempt you to say, "It wasn't my fault! I couldn't help it." But the blame game only nurtures the fallacy that control of your financial future is with someone other than you. Thousands of persons have used blame as an excuse for their poverty: the government didn't help them enough, they didn't have the right education, their spouse let them down. The list is endless.

Your financial freedom starts and ends with you. You have everything you need to start on this exciting path. Success never happens until *you* make it happen, and you make good things happen when you make a decision to move forward. Yes, your decisions will involve risks. Yes, your decisions will bring more uncertainty. But only by making daring decisions will you ever succeed. Success is no accident. Success is not a coincidence. Success is a commitment. Today is a great day to decide where you want to be five, ten, twenty years from today.

Examine your personal situation now by making a list of all the possible excuses you have consciously or unconsciously made that allowed you to take on too much debt or held you back from your financial dreams. Here are a few examples to jog your thinking:

- I have four children and a wife to support, feed, house, and educate. I'm already working 60 hours a week!

- I am poor and uneducated and living in the inner city where I face prejudice and subhuman living conditions.

- My parents didn't plan for their retirement and I have to support them.

- I am disabled and cannot support myself.

- My ex-wife takes every extra cent I make.

Your list will reflect your attitude about yourself and others. As a professional motivator for more than 40 years, I can tell you without a doubt that your situation will *never change*, until you change your *attitude*!

Take a serious look at your list of excuses. Perhaps this is the first time you've realized that an excuse is holding you back, that a problem is controlling your financial future. Are you really willing to surrender control of your life and your future to these problems? We all have difficulties. We all have problems. But only when you are willing to rise to the challenge and change your attitude will you begin to succeed. Every problem is a possibility in disguise. Every obstacle is an opportunity.

Today is the day to make a decision to take responsibility for your own future, a decision to succeed despite your problems, a decision to leave the excuses behind, a decision to commit to financial freedom.

Are you ready to take responsibility for your financial future? If so, you are ready to take the first step up the ladder of financial success. I suggest you not only commit to the following affirmation, but attach it to your refrigerator. Clip it to your checkbook. Tape it on your computer. Live it with your actions!

Affirmation: *Today, I accept full responsibility for my financial position. I know I am the only one who can change my future. I realize financial success is not an accident—it is a commitment. Today, I commit myself to financial freedom!*

Step Two: Itemize Your Assets

"Beginning is half done!"

Many books on personal finance will tell you to itemize your assets. But I know of no book on personal finance that suggests you to do it the way we will. Although getting a clear understanding of your financial situation is key to taking positive steps toward financial freedom, it is not as important as understanding your greatest asset: YOU. You should itemize not only your financial holdings, but your hidden, underused, undiscovered talents and assets as well.

Venita Van Caspel, a dear friend of mine and a member of my International Board, is one of the most successful financial advisors in the world. Her books on financial planning have repeatedly been bestsellers. But the talents she has did not come out until she faced the devastating tragedy of her husband's death in a plane accident. She knew she could not afford to lose the small insurance settlement she received. She returned to college, studied investments, and received a degree in finance. When she learned that only 2 percent of people retire financially independent, she determined to make a difference. She has made it her mission to teach people how to make the best use of their financial resources. In addition, she became the first woman to own a seat on the Pacific Coast Stock Exchange. She turned her experience into a profitable and rewarding profession.

What experiences have you had that form a hidden valuable asset? What knowledge do you have that is of use to you and others? What talent did you once take great pride in, only to let it sit on the shelf unused?

Before you itemize your finances, look at those hidden assets that you may have overlooked. These are the assets that will determine your future. You may be richer than you think.

First, let's not forget our freedom. If you live in America or another free country, you have tremendous freedom that people have been willing to die for. Let's never forget our freedom as one of our greatest assets!

Second, no matter where you live, you have access to an incredible amount of free education. Adult community college courses, libraries, college courses that can be audited, and surfing the Internet are all resources that, if not free, are so inexpensive that you cannot afford not to take advantage of them. The ability to educate yourself, even in your home, is one of the greatest assets we have in today's world.

Third, social and community groups offer many programs and educational activities. Your church or synagogue is a tremendous asset to assist you in discovering your God-given talents. As a grandparent, I am constantly amazed at the talent that I see in each of my 17 grandchildren. My daughter will say to me, "Oh, I think Jennie has great athletic ability. She could become a professional athlete someday." Or my son will say, "Bobby is a great musician. He has such potential, Dad."

Isn't it sad that as we get older, we tend to quit saying to ourselves, "Gee, you have great artistic potential" or "You should keep up with your studies because you are so smart!" Somehow, we have allowed ourselves to believe that if we had a hidden talent it would have come out by the time we were adults. Or we believe we have achieved our full potential. But the truth is, each of us has only begun to reveal our true potential.

Get out that pad of paper again and list your unrealized personal assets. Take a look at yourself and ask these questions:

- What education do I have that I have not used fully?
- What experiences that have shaped my life can be used as an asset?
- What interests did I have as a child that I never fully developed? Can those interests point to a hidden talent?
- What support groups do I have that are an incredible asset to me: my family? my church? my friendships?

Now that you have taken inventory of your asset potential, let's take an inventory of your dollars, using the Personal Financial Statement worksheet on the following page. It does no good to have your head buried in the sand. You need to know if you have a money problem—but remember, "*You don't have a money problem—you have an idea problem!*" We will deal more with that later, but first, we need to know how much of a money problem you have. Only then can you come up with an idea big enough to stretch your creative powers to the fullest!

Before you assume you don't have enough money, decide to get more mileage out of what you do have. Learn to stretch your money, much as you would get the last dab of toothpaste from the tube.

PERSONAL FINANCIAL STATEMENT

Fill in this Personal Financial Statement. Total the amount of your assets and subtract that from the total amount of your liabilities. The result will be equal to your net worth.

ASSETS		LIABILITIES	
Checking Accounts	________	Mortgages	________
Savings Accounts	________	Credit Cards	________
Money Market Accounts	________	Bank Cards	________
Certificate of Deposits	________	Department Store	________
Mutual Funds	________	Gasoline	________
Stocks and Bonds	________	Other	________
Savings Bonds	________	*Total Credit Cards*	________
Total Liquid Assets	________		
		Personal Loans	
Personal Assets		Education	________
Home	________	Automobile	________
Personal Property	________	Finance Companies	________
Autos	________	Total Personal Loans	________
Other	________	Miscellaneous Loans	________
	________	TOTAL LIABILITIES	________
	________		
Total Personal Assets	________	**Personal Net Worth**	
		Total Assets	________
Retirement Accounts	________	Minus Total Liabilities	________
TOTAL ASSETS	________	NET WORTH	________

MONTHLY INCOME & EXPENSES

It is also important to get a handle on your monthly expenses in relation to your monthly income. To do so, fill out this worksheet. Be sure to include any large payments you receive throughout the year as an adjusted monthly income amount. For example, if you receive a $1,200 payment on an annual basis, account for it as $100 per month. Conversely, if you have just purchased a new couch on a six-month plan with no money down, be sure to include that liability on your monthly expense statement.

MONTHLY INCOME

Paycheck(s) __________

Rental Income __________

Dividends __________

Interest Income __________

Miscellaneous __________

Total Monthly Income __________

MONTHLY EXPENSES

Housing (Rent or Mortgage Payment) __________

Insurance

– Home __________

– Car __________

– Medical __________

– Rental __________

Food __________

Entertainment __________

Clothing __________

Education __________

Medical/Dental __________

Subscriptions __________

Travel __________

Home Maintenance __________

Gasoline __________

Laundry/Dry Cleaning __________

Total Monthly Expenses __________

Total Monthly Income __________

Minus Total Expenses __________

MONTHLY TOTAL __________

In order to take the first steps down the road to financial freedom, it is essential that your income exceeds your outgo (expenses) or it will be the upstart of your downfall!

Management is taking control of a situation in which you will be held accountable for the results. Your financial freedom is dependent upon your ability to exercise leadership to reshape, reorganize, and retool your future. It takes time to change the course of a ship, and it may take time to realize your goals, but it can happen!

Are you ready to manage your assets? Are you willing to take leadership of your skills and talents? Are you committed to unveiling the greatest resource available to you—your God-given intellect, your hard earned experiences, and your creative energies? *You are the greatest asset you have!*

This second step up the ladder of financial freedom is a foundational building block that gives knowledge and confidence upon which you can dream your dreams. Once you know who you are and what you have to work with, you can decide to go anywhere you want! Beginning is half done! This is just the beginning. This is the start of a fascinating adventure.

Affirmation: *I will dig deeply to discover my hidden talents and abilities as I seek to itemize not only my financial assets, but my God-given assets. I am committed to take control and manage myself and my finances wisely, and to use my resources completely and confidently. I have great resources upon which to draw.*

Step Three: Visualize Your Objectives

"Plan your work, then work your plan."

Congratulations! You've taken the first steps. You have taken full responsibility for where you are and you have a clear understanding of your financial and personal assets. Now, you're ready for the fun part. The challenge. The dreams. The goals.

It's time to believe in yourself and your dream. But simply believing in yourself without positive action is fruitless. You must have a plan and you must work that plan! Remember, if you fail to plan you are planning to fail.

A financial plan is like the blueprints for a house. A house must be constructed carefully, with the knowledge of a contractor and architect to ensure a secure foundation. Likewise your financial plan needs to be constructed carefully on the basis of sound financial advice or a model you can follow.

First, visualize your objectives. What does financial freedom mean to you? What are your financial goals? Here are some possibilities.

1. ***To be debt free.*** For some this goal seems like an impossibility, especially when you look at your financial worksheet. Perhaps your debts are so great they are weighing down all other hopes and dreams. Simply to get out of debt would be a dream come true. But no matter how impossible this objective seems, it is the key to financial freedom for you and your family. It is an objective of all possibility thinkers who still have some debt.

2. ***To retire in dignity.*** Notice I did not say you should have as an objective to live on a cruise ship six months out of the year. But to retire in dignity is a moral and God-given right. The alternative is to spend your final years in poverty, dependent upon the government or your children. I firmly believe that God's plan for your life includes the freedom to live with dignity in your golden years.

   You might say, "I can retire in dignity. But I want to retire in luxury!" If that is what you want to strive for, that too is possible. But there will be a price for the reward.

3. ***To provide for my children's higher education.*** College tuition has soared. Private colleges remain out of reach for many families. However, with planning, savings, and enough time, tuition at any school is attainable.

No matter what your financial objectives, set them now! Time is your greatest ally when it comes to financial planning. The more time you have to act on your goals, the less risk and rate of return it requires to achieve it. No matter what your objective, get started! More people are financial failures for lack of goal setting than for any other reason. Their lack of financial goals leaves them to the whims and wishes of the moment.

In setting your goals, include a deadline, a time by when you want to accomplish each goal. Then set intermediate goals so that you will know if you are on the right track.

If your main objective is financial freedom, there are great resources that will equip you with the tools to achieve your goals. Read as much as you can, including such national publications as *The Wall Street Journal*, *Investor's Business Daily*, and *Barron's Weekly* and such magazines as *Money*, *Worth*, *Forbes*, and *Fortune*. Get in the habit of reading the business section of your local newspaper. Go to the library and check the financial section for worthy books, including Venita Van Caspel's *Money Dynamics for the 1990s* (Simon and Schuster), *Smart Money* by Ken and Daria Dolan (Random House), *How to Make Money in Stocks* by William O'Neill (McGraw Hill), *One Up on Wall Street* by Peter Lynch (Simon and Schuster), *The Templeton Touch* by Sir John Templeton (Doubleday), and *Financial Peace* by Dave Ramsey (LAMPO Press). Stock market investing, college investing, and owning your own home are all worthy goals that can be realized with the needed expertise.

Once you determine your objective, you need to *commit yourself* to your goal. Many reasons will come up, both worthwhile and obscure, that will tempt you to get sidetracked from your objectives. Financial emergencies can bombard your carefully planned budgets. I can guarantee that you will meet obstacles to your financial objectives. That is why your commitment must be in place. Commitment keeps you moving forward even when obstacles arise.

You also must visualize your objectives in specific, concrete terms. You must see yourself in this new dream. My friend Zig Ziglar, a motivational genius, often tells the story of the man who desires a new boat. He really doesn't take much time to think about the details of the boat. He just knows that he wants a new boat. The odds are great that this man will never get his boat. Another man also wants a boat. But unlike the first man, he knows exactly what make and model of boat he wants. He knows the details of the finish, the woodwork, the size of the engine, the number of passengers it can hold, the fabric color of the cushions. He even has a name picked out for his dream boat. This man will achieve his goal. Why? Because he can see it. He can hear it. He can even smell it!

Today, really visualize your objectives. Make a complete list. Don't just write down "college education," but list the name of the college and find out what the tuition is. Be specific on where you want to vacation and how much the airfare and hotel will cost. Ask your spouse what his or her dreams are and specify them as well. And when you list your retirement needs, make sure you are fully informed as to what the costs will be based on where you want to retire. *If you can dream it—you can do it!*

Affirmation: *I have dreams and goals that are important to me and my family. These dreams are important enough that I will spend the time and energy to fully visualize them—detail by detail. When I dream my dreams, they won't be in black and white—they will be in vivid color! I have exciting and worthy dreams!*

Step Four: Prioritize Your Spending

"Measure three times, but cut only once."

The proverb of the old Russian tailor is great advice when it comes to allocating your finances. Imagine that you have just the right amount of yardage of a very precious fabric to create a garment that will become a family heirloom. There is not enough material for leftover scraps. You are allowed no waste. You must measure carefully before you cut.

So it is with your financial resources. You have a certain amount of earning years that will enable you to create your family nest egg. Your annual expenses are much like patterns that need to fit within the framework. You can't afford to waste your money. If your outflow of expenses exceeds your income, it will be the upstart of your downfall.

Once you have determined all of your assets and all of your current liabilities, you need to develop a detailed record of your spending habits. Start by keeping a record for one month of everything you spend. Unfortunately, many people are caught in a spiral of spending that seems, at best, reckless. Until you write it down, you probably won't even know where your cash is flowing. And it does flow!

There are many ways to record your expenses. Computer programs such as *Quicken* enable you to list all of your checks and cash purchases and will track your financial activity in detailed reports. If you do not feel comfortable with a computer, you may prefer keeping track of your spending in a three-ring binder. Some people carry a small notebook with them and record their spending in it.

Once you have a record of where you spend your money over a month, compare it with your income. To become debt-free, to accomplish your objectives, to fulfill your dreams, you need to bring in more money than you spend. In the short run, it is far easier to cut your spending than to increase your income. Review carefully where you are spending your money to see where you can cut back. Use the spending record to establish a budget.

Add up your pennies

It's amazing how quickly one can get "dollared to death." A good friend of mine regularly stops at a gourmet coffee store each morning before work for two cappuccinos and two rolls for himself and his wife. He recently told me that he budgets $3,000 a year for this luxury! It's fine to do so if you are aware of where your money is going. However, when it was pointed out to another friend who had trouble meeting his car payments of $280 per month that he was spending $160 a month in his morning visits to the coffee store, he was amazed and quickly changed his habits.

A carpooling mother recently complained that she was fed up with having to spend $10 each afternoon to stop by a convenience store to feed drinks and snacks to four hungry kids. At three times a week, she was spending $120 a month without realizing it! She quickly decided that she could provide snacks and drinks from home for a fraction of the cost.

Patch your pockets

All of us have holes in our pockets. The key is to find out where the holes are and to patch them quickly. Keep detailed spending ledgers. Review your receipts and expenses from last year. What purchases did you make that you regret or were unnecessary? What impulsive spending did you give in to? Cut the fat out of your spending habits for leaner and cleaner monthly living.

Here are a few simple ways to stitch up the holes in your pockets:

- Don't buy impulsively. Plan purchases in advance by using a shopping list and sticking to it.

- Use coupons whenever possible.

- Keep receipts and record all purchases.

- Give gifts of time and talent rather than purchased gifts.

- Buy in bulk items that are not perishable.

- Wait for sales. Ask retailers when they will have a sale because they often plan sales well in advance.

Cost compare everything

When shopping for a house, most people spend endless weekends driving through neighborhoods, scouring the newspaper, and negotiating the selling price. However, when shopping for a mortgage, those same buyers skip the shopping phase and regrettably overpay for one of the biggest purchases of their lives. A mortgage mistake can cost you from $100 to $3,000 annually, and $4,000 to $120,000 or more during your lifetime. While you are probably ready and willing to negotiate on the price of a home, be aware that you can negotiate the mortgage as well. If you are financing or refinancing a home, here are some mortgage shopping strategies:

- Don't necessarily follow your realtor's advice regarding lenders. Instead, consult a newspaper that publishes complete and current lists of mortgage rates.

- Consider a shorter term mortgage, such as a 15- or 20-year loan instead of a 30-year one. The savings in interest will astound you and you will own your home outright in half the time.

- Compare the interest rate, how often the rate can change, the "cap," or limit to which the interest rate can increase, the index to which the interest rate is tied, how often monthly payments can change, and whether there is a negative amortization or balloon payment.

- Don't back away from a lower interest rate loan because the points are higher. Remember, points are deductible from your federal income tax in the year of closing, and if you plan to keep the house long term, the lower interest rate will pay off.

Buy for best value

If ever you should measure three times but cut only once, it is with the purchase of an automobile. When you consider what the car will cost, include not just the buying price of the car, but also the cost of maintenance and insurance combined with the hidden cost of depreciation. Be sure that the car you buy is the car you need. Too often our insatiable appetites for newer and better things entice us to purchase something we probably can't afford.

If you are going to purchase a car, ask yourself these questions: What do I really need? What price am I willing to pay? Will a used car do? Should I save and pay cash? If I am buying on credit, what can I really afford? Should I lease rather than buy? What are the insurance rates on the various cars I am considering?

Remember, paying cash for a used car is the most economical way to go. A new car will depreciate 20 percent the minute you drive it off the lot. Interest on an auto loan will escalate the cost quickly. If you must finance, make as big a down payment as possible, and try to prepay the loan at an accelerated rate.

Prioritize, Prioritize, Prioritize!

It can't be said enough: Prioritize your expenses! Cut out those that have a low priority. The path to financial freedom always stops at this crossroads. Are you going to stay true to the dreams that you visualized earlier? Are you committed to your goals? Are you planning your work and working your plan? Then keep your priorities. Unless you do, your plans will crumble.

Measure three times. Prioritize when you pay the bills. Prioritize where you spend your money when you shop. Prioritize your goals when you have an impulse. Does a particular purchase fit with your goals? Does it meet your objectives? Can you achieve the same thing at less cost? Can you find it cheaper somewhere else? Have you exhausted all the possibilities? Have you remained committed to your desire for financial freedom?

Now, cut only once. Bring the credit card out slowly. Write the check confidently. Pay the bill happily—because you know it is the right thing to do!

Affirmation: *I am committed to my financial freedom. That is why I will be confident each time I make a purchase that it is the right one. If I have reservations, I will wait. If I'm not sure, I will examine it more closely. I will stick with my priorities. I will measure three times—and cut only once!*

Step Five: Scrutinize Your Values

"Earn more—or want less."

Financial happiness does not always depend on having more money. Financial happiness does depend, however, on having enough money for what you want. If you are not happy with your financial situation, there are two obvious choices: earn more or want less.

Earn More

Right about now you are possibly thinking, "Wait a minute! I'm retired. I'm on a fixed income. How can I earn more?" or "I'm still in school. I have to attend classes full time. How can I earn more?" or possibly, "I'm working full time already. There is no way I can take on a second (or third) job!"

Stop! Recognize these comments as a common negative reaction. Now, put it aside. I am convinced that no matter what you are doing to earn an income, you can do it better or do more of it. If you are retired, you have a great deal of time available to you that is a precious commodity to people without time on their hands. There are many ways you can market your time and experiences. I know many students who have not only worked full time in class, but have carried two or three part time jobs. Of course they were tired, but they were paying the price to further their education and realize their dreams. You don't have a money problem—you have an idea problem!

Expand your education

Remember that asset list we developed at the beginning of this chapter of the undiscovered, under-utilized, undeveloped talents and interests you have? This may be the time for you to review that list and ask yourself, "If I further my education in this field, can I increase my income?" For some, the answer will be yes. Perhaps you still need to complete your high school education. Perhaps you began your college education but never finished. Would an advanced degree in your field help you earn more? Education is an excellent way to increase your earning potential. It may take a few years, but nothing great is ever achieved without paying a price. The rewards in personal fulfillment may be all the extra income you need!

Many mothers are returning to school after raising their children. Cory SerVaas is a prime example. After her children were in school, she decided to become a medical doctor. For her, that meant going back to college to complete her undergraduate work, four years of medical school, and residency. She studied alongside her children. Today, she is a respected physician. She is also editor of the *Saturday Evening Post.*

Maximize production

Have you done the best with what you have? Are you working as hard as you can? A member of my church, Gary Franken, amazes me and everyone who knows him. He uses a wheelchair due to cerebral palsy. His lack of control over his muscles and nervous system make his movements jerky. When he talks, his slurred words make it difficult to understand, but the smile on his face encourages you to listen. Gary never accepted the negative predictions that the experts made about him. Instead, he worked hard to pursue his dreams. First he learned to walk. Then he learned to drive. He developed his mind. Today, he is the Associate Transportation Planner in charge of long-range planning for the California State Department of Transportation. He has squeezed so much from so little. What would the world be like if we all were more like Gary Franken and did the best with what we had?

Never reject an idea because "I don't have the time." You will make time for what is important to you. Scrutinize your values. Focus on your goals. Manage others to free up your time for what is really important to you. Wise time management can turn impossibilities into possibilities, every time!

Consider relocation

Review your goals, your dreams, your assets. Are you in the location you should be to attain them? Perhaps you need to relocate. I was a young man in college when I first toured Southern California. The blue skies, warm temperatures, and orange groves tempted me to stay. Instead, I finished my schooling in Michigan and took my first church in Illinois. Yet always in the back of my mind was California. I *knew* that was where I needed to be to build the church of my dreams. When the time came, I moved with my wife and two children, and with $500 to pursue my dream. It was the right move for me. Are you where you need to be?

Want Less

Maybe your problem is not that you don't have enough money, but that you want too much of the wrong thing. This is not a contradiction to possibility thinking. The saddest funeral I ever conducted was for a very wealthy man. He did not have a single mourner at his funeral! He had three sons who lived in the community, but they did not attend. His ex-wife did not attend. None of his business associates attended. I was astounded. I asked the mortician to explain. The funeral director said, "All he wanted was to make more money and acquire more toys. He didn't have time for his children or his wife. He didn't have time or money for his church or charities. He died an extremely sick and lonely man."

That, my friend, is failure! It is failure not to value the precious commodities of family and friends. How do you keep a balance and maintain equilibrium? It is difficult because our society tells us that happiness comes from material things. We are seduced by consumerism. Maintaining a balance requires a constant vigilance to keep your priorities straight, constantly critical of the allure of consumerism. My friend Bob Buford wrote a dynamic book called *Half Time* (Zondervan) in which he challenges one to live not only a successful life, but a significant one. In doing so, he says, one often needs to downsize.

"When Thoreau moved into a cabin on Walden Pond, he lightened up on the non-essentials in life. Think about all the time and energy that are drained by owning a boat, a cottage, a second or third car, or a country club membership. None of these things are bad by themselves and are, in fact, designed to provide some fun in life. But they can very easily become master controllers. Most people I know who own a boat feel they have to use it to make it a worthwhile investment. I also know people who do not particularly enjoy spending four hours on a golf course but do so because they belong to a club. If these kinds of things are preventing you from regaining control of your life, get rid of them."

There is a struggle going on today within working families regarding whether to sacrifice the mother's time at home in order to get additional income. The choices we make reflect the values to which we commit. Many families have found they have been happier with less income and with mother at home. Some working women have elected to stay home during the years when their children are infants and toddlers. Others have managed on less income while working at home. Other families have relocated to a less costly place to live in order to attain their goals.

In today's world, you will be confronted with innumerable demands on your time, energy, thoughts, and money. Your greatest temptation will be from things that are good. But take caution. Don't sacrifice the greater good for the lesser good. Don't choose to live a mediocre, "good" life instead of an excellent one. Don't take the easy goal instead of the impossible challenge.

Want less—less stress, less worry, less conflict, less mediocrity!

Bring your values in line with your goals. Bring your values in line with your beliefs. Then bring your spending in line with your values. Don't assume you are living your life the best way just because you've always lived it this way! Don't think you are on the right track just because it is the same track your neighbor is on. Don't follow the crowd to financial hardship by forgetting what you really value. Scrutinize each and every value you hold dear. Are you in line with your spiritual commitments? Your family commitments? Your commitments to the community around you? When your values are secure and your spending reflects those values, you will be on the solid ground needed for financial happiness.

Isn't it amazing how many people fail to even consider this important rung up the ladder to financial freedom? I'm sure you will take this step confidently and securely.

Affirmation: I know what I believe. I know why I believe it. I know how to live my life based on those beliefs. I am committed to ensuring that my financial habits and spending patterns accurately reflect my deeply rooted values.

Step Six: Overcome Your Obstacles One at a Time

"God and I are greater than my problems."

In the previous chapter we told of President John F. Kennedy's call to Walter Burke, chairman of the board of McDonnell Douglas Corporation, to ask for his help to accomplish the impossible task of putting a man on the moon. "We both know that's impossible," said Kennedy. "Now let's figure out a way to make it possible." And they did. Years later I asked Walter Burke how he tackled such an impossible assignment. His answer was brilliant. "I learned many years ago," he said, "that one large problem is really a collection of little problems. The way to tackle an impossible problem is to break it down and solve the several little problems, one at a time."

As you face the challenge of achieving financial freedom by becoming debt free, it is tempting to think of the challenge as one huge, impossible, insurmountable problem. As long as you think of it that way and look for one answer to such a big problem, it will be impossible. But the minute you break down the challenge of achieving financial freedom into a number of small challenges, you have made the impossible possible. You will realize that you can accomplish the small challenges and you will do it.

Today is a great day to identify the smaller challenges that will lead you and your family to financial freedom. Then put into practice one by one those plans that will overcome your obstacles and meet your challenges. If you suffer from unmanageable debt, if you cannot pay more than the minimum on your credit cards, if you seem unable to stretch your paycheck to cover your monthly expenses, then you need quickly to begin to overcome your obstacles one at a time. Time will work for you or against you.

You will need to identify the smaller challenges that will lead to the accomplishment of your larger goal. Each of us will have different challenges. But here are a few suggestions. No one of these will solve your entire problem. But all together—and by tackling the smaller challenges you have identified for yourself—they will help put you on the road to success.

Get out of the plastic trap

The ability to pull out a credit card at the mall or at lunch is a manageable luxury for the disciplined. However, for too many of us, plastic is a disaster waiting to happen. For the worst offenders, "plastic surgery" is in order. Cut up those credit cards. Don't be fooled into thinking that you can afford an item just because a bank is willing to loan you the money. The interest will consume you.

For those more disciplined, living in a credit card society takes careful precautionary measures to ensure that the credit you establish monthly can be paid off monthly. Limit yourself to one or two credit cards. Many banks and financial institutions want the privilege—and the profit—of lending money to you. It's a competitive environment. Make sure you have shopped for a low-fee or no-fee card. Switch to cards offering a lower interest rate. Many banks will transfer a balance from one card to another.

If you are able to handle a credit card, but often are surprised by the monthly balance, start to keep a register of your purchases. Some people find it helpful to deduct each purchase from their checkbook, even though the payment won't be made until the following month. One friend physically writes out a check to the credit card company every time she makes a purchase on her card. She still gets the airline miles, but without any surprises at the end of the month.

Finally, if you have any money in a savings account, pay off the balance on your credit card. The money in a savings account offering only 3 to 4 percent works harder for you if it is paying off a balance on which you are paying an interest rate of 14 to 18 percent. But don't let such a strategy of paying off your credit card lead you to believe you can build up your credit card debt again. Next time you won't have the savings account to pay it off.

Minimize mall malady

"Meet me at the mall for lunch." It sounds innocent enough. But how often have you had lunch and then decided to stroll the shops "for a second." Forty-five dollars later and carrying your new find, you return home or to the office unaware that you have just succumbed to mall malady. Retailers have succeeded. You have lost. Whereas many purchases will fit your budget, frequent mall shoppers will admit that most do not.

Minimize the amount of time you spend in a mall. Don't be fooled into thinking you can innocently stroll through the mall for a recreational pastime. It will cost you! The displays, the music, the excitement of beautifully clothed salespeople asking if they can help you, all relax your senses, including your financial freedom radar, which should be sharp and aware at the mall. Your values, your goals, your assets, your personal responsibility are all under attack. Keep focused. If you are there for lunch, then enjoy your lunch. If you are there for a specific purchase, enjoy the shopping for that purchase. But be aware of the not so subtle pressures encouraging you to part with your hard earned money. Even if you realize you are not too fond of a particular purchase, you might end up keeping it because you don't want to find the receipt, go "all the way back to the mall," and hassle the parking to return the item. Be smart. Be alert. Then enjoy yourself.

Turn that dial

Not too long ago, the only way a retailer could come to your house was through a very expensive direct mail piece or a salesman knocking at your door. Such approaches were infrequent and not too difficult to resist. Today, your home is open to any retailer through television and the Internet. While shopping on the Internet may not be fully established, cable shopping programs certainly are! Items that you might easily pass by at a store suddenly come to life through handsomely produced television programs. Soft-spoken salespeople convince you of the beauty and value of a special item. The sales price, often slashed in half from the "retail" price gives the impression of value and cements the sale. You pick up the phone and you give your credit card number. Hopefully, when the item comes you will be pleased.

Are you able to resist the allure of the television solicitations or are you succumbing to their proven sales tactics? If this is an area of temptation for you, turn that dial! Don't let the salespeople pretend to be your best friend. Usually we watch television shopping programs because we don't have anything else to do. Don't give up your financial freedom because of a few moments of loneliness. Understand why you're watching in the first place.

Forget about the Joneses

Although we hate to admit it, we are all influenced by what our neighbors, co-workers, boss, friends, and extended family own and the things on which they spend their money. We wouldn't be the social creatures we are if we didn't have a competitive nature urging us to do better than others. But for some people, this is a real trap. Your neighbor may drive home with a new luxury automobile and park it in his driveway, and then has the nerve to wax it each weekend in front of you! Your best friend may show up for dinner in a terrific outfit, and you realize that you have never seen her in the same outfit twice. And your closet has "nothing" in it. Or your computer friend may upgrade weekly with the newest technological gadget, leaving you feeling as if your laptop is a dinosaur.

We all have pressures to keep up with the Joneses and the Mitchells and the Smiths. But these pressures will cause you to stray from the path to financial freedom. Do you really believe that with their impulsive spending patterns, the Joneses, Mitchells, or Smiths have any reliable financial goals? This is an opportunity to keep the commitment you made earlier. These pressures will tempt you to abandon your dreams. Think about it. Who are you trying to keep up with? You might be surprised by your answer.

■ ■ ■

Take the time to list the personal pitfalls that continuously rob you of your financial freedom. Your list might reflect some of the excuses that you listed at the beginning of this chapter. You might accurately say that some of these are out of your control, but you might also acknowledge that you can control many of these pitfalls. Remember what Walter Burke said to me: "One large problem is really a collection of little problems. Break it down and solve the several little problems, one at a time."

Apply this principle to your goal of financial freedom today! Break the problem down into little parts. You cannot solve the entire situation at once. But have heart. Stay firm. Keep focused on your goals and do not succumb to the pressures that are always around you. When you begin to see that your problem is made up of little parts, you'll begin to realize that you are bigger than your problem!

Affirmation: *I am convinced that I can solve my problems—each small part at a time. I will stand firm in my resolve toward financial freedom. I know that no problem is bigger than I am—with God's help!*

Step Seven: Make Your Money Work for You

"It will work—if I work it!"

One of my favorite stories is that of the little boy who wanted to be rich when he grew up. He decided the best way to learn how to become rich was to ask someone who was. He noticed a man who drove an expensive car and always parked at a construction site down the road. One day, the boy went up to the man and asked, "Excuse me, sir, but can you tell me how to be rich like you when I grow up?"

Impressed with the young boy's ambition, the man said, "Simple, son. Buy a red shirt and work like it all depends on you." The puzzled boy asked the man to explain. "You see," he said, "I am a developer. I buy property, build buildings, and sell them. When I started out, I decided that if I wanted to get ahead, I would have to work a little harder than everybody else. I did a little better job, got to work a little earlier, and stayed a little longer. But I also decided my efforts should be noticed. All the workers wore blue shirts with blue overalls. So I bought a red shirt. The boss noticed me and I was rewarded! That's my advice to you, son."

Your continued climb up the ladder of financial freedom depends on one person alone—you. You can be debt free, you can have financial freedom, if you work hard, mobilize your resources, and stay committed to your dreams.

Today, you are ready to learn how to make your money work hardest—for you! You've recognized your responsibility, itemized your assets, visualized your objectives, prioritized your spending, scrutinized your values, and overcome your obstacles one at a time. Now you are ready for the next step on the road to financial freedom: Take care of the financial fundamentals.

Pay off highest interest debt first

Let's assume that you have a little money ready to save, but you still have not paid off all of your high interest credit cards or other high interest debt. Unless you are an investment whiz who can easily earn more than 20 percent a year on your money, it makes sense to pay off the high interest debt. The compounding debt will eat up your savings account before you are able to earn the 3 or 4 percent it pays. When you are out from under the monthly interest expense, you will be able to quickly add to your savings account again.

Establish an emergency savings account

Once you have paid down all of your high interest debt, not including your monthly mortgage, and you are keeping your monthly expenses in check with your financial goals, you need to establish what I call an emergency savings account. Accidents and emergencies can seriously sidetrack your financial objectives if you are unprepared. However, with an emergency savings account, your financial dreams can stand up to the unexpected blows. A sudden layoff or financial illness can occur any time. Therefore, you need to have a savings account that can step up to pay your monthly mortgage and living expenses during your business or medical recovery.

Ideally, you should set aside six months of your bare, basic monthly expenses. This savings should be invested in a liquid money market account or a basic savings account at a bank. It should be insured and easily accessed—but only for emergencies. An emergency is something that *drastically* affects your financial income or expenses beyond your control.

Protect yourself with insurance

You *must* have adequate health insurance for you and your family. This is not a luxury. It is a necessity. I am constantly surprised by the attitude that "I can't afford health insurance." Yet that same person can afford to dress nicely and eat out occasionally. Undeniably, health insurance is expensive, but it is a necessity. Don't ever think of going even a month without health or automobile insurance. Perhaps you cannot afford it, but you cannot afford to be without it. Make sure, however, that the insurance you have is the insurance you need. Insurance is not meant to cover small financial inconveniences, just major claims. You can save money on health, automobile, and most other kinds of insurance by getting a high deductible. This means that you will pay for small claims, but the insurance company gives you a break because it has less work and fewer claims to deal with.

When you shop for insurance, carefully evaluate your needs because your need for insurance changes over the years, and you should be sure that you are not paying for insurance you no longer need. Insurance on the life of the family's breadwinner is important for families with small children. But if your children are grown and you and your spouse are comfortable with your savings, your need for life insurance is minimal.

Review your insurance needs with a qualified insurance agent. Make sure you have enough insurance so that if you do have a catastrophe, you won't be ruined.

■ ■ ■

Once you have reached the rung of financial success that includes an emergency savings account, adequate health and life insurance, and all your high interest debts have been paid off, then you are truly on the path toward financial freedom.

Make your money work hardest for you! You worked hard to get to this point. You have made the tough choices. You have set your financial plans in progress. You are on the road to financial security. You have protected yourself against disaster. You are taking each step up the ladder of financial freedom with confidence. Congratulations!

Affirmation: *I have come this far with faith—faith that I can make my financial future one filled with freedom. I will continue to make my money work hardest for me and my family. Only then will I have the freedom to follow my dreams.*

Step Eight: Organize Your Network

"When you have exhausted all possibilities, remember, you haven't!"

Achieving financial freedom is a long-term project. Like a beautiful piece of embroidery, it takes patience and persistence to complete. And if you are like most people, you cannot and will not do it alone. It will require the help, advice, and assistance of financial advisors, investment counselors, attorneys, and friends to achieve financial freedom.

I'll never forget a trip to China I made many years ago. While there, I watched remarkable weavers at work. At one factory, I saw weavers working on a carpet that had been in progress for more than twenty-two years. It was estimated that it would take another fifteen or twenty years to complete it. Imagine what a great work of art that will be!

Likewise, your financial path is a work of art that will take time and the help of a network of people who are able and willing to help you. Your attitude toward financial freedom is a lifetime commitment. You are developing a new pattern of living. This life pattern will steadily and slowly emerge as you make decisions, spot opportunities, and solve problems. Now is the time to expand your network of professionals who can assist you in your financial goals, whether it is restructuring your debt or planning your investments. They are probably there already, just waiting for you to discover them. Here are some great places to start looking.

Non-profit financial counseling centers

If you are at the point on the financial ladder where you are still struggling with an overload of debt and need additional support, there are many financial counseling programs available for you. Many universities, local courts, churches, credit unions and banks, and housing authorities offer such services for little or no fee. If you are having difficulty paying your debts, such services will assist in establishing debt repayment plans that include paying the program a certain amount each month, which is then distributed among your lenders. Most often, the lenders themselves will pay the fees to aid you in paying back your debts.

Other non-profit consumer advocacy groups offer members legal advice to educate and protect clients from unfair practices in the credit system. Some of the services you can receive include IRS negotiation, mortgage prequalification, and local attorney referrals. But be aware that there are some fraudulent "credit clinics" that run scams. As always, be informed. Educate yourself. Before getting too involved with a credit counselor or repayment program, check references. Consult the Better Business Bureau. Ask the service for names of people it has helped or businesses with whom it has worked.

Finally, if continued debt is a constant struggle, I highly recommend Debtors Anonymous, which is based on the same premise as Alcoholics Anonymous. It is a national support group that helps compulsive spenders overcome their addiction. Check your local directory for a chapter in your community or write to: Debtors Anonymous, General Service Office, P.O. Box 20322, New York, NY 10025-9992.

Two organizations worthy of your attention are: North American Consumer Alliance, 6911 South 1300 East, Suite 500, Midvale, UT 84047, (800) 497-NACA; and Consumer Credit Counseling Service. Call 800-388-CCCS for the office nearest you.

Perhaps you are not in need of services such as those which will help you with debt restructuring. But no matter what your financial condition, you need to organize your network to include assistance with your financial investments and planning. Such assistance may be as close as your workplace.

Employee sponsored savings accounts

Many employees sponsor savings and investment accounts such as a 401K program and will automatically deduct an amount of money from the employee's paycheck. The employer will often match a certain percentage of the employee's investment. If this program is available to you, do it! It is an excellent benefit.

Investment clubs

Investment clubs are a great place for beginning investors. A typical club usually consists of other beginning investors who each contribute a specified amount of money, such as $25 or $30 a month, to be invested in stocks. The club members then research stocks together and try to analyze the economic conditions that would affect their chosen stocks. The group then votes on which stocks to buy or sell. The experience gained will become an invaluable part of your investment knowledge. When you decide to leave the club, you will receive your prorated share of the investments. To find our about investment clubs in your area, or to start a club of your own, contact: The National Association of Investor Corporations, 1515 East 11th Mile Road, Royal Oak, MI 48067, (313) 543-0612.

Financial planners

Many employers provide personal financial planning services for their top personnel. You may not have this luxury, but such a benefit indicates how important these companies think sound financial planning is. You should find a financial planner who will earn his or her compensation from either commissions, fees, or a combination of both. A Certified Financial Planner can assist you in tax planning, comprehensive investment planning, retirement and estate planning, risk management, and business planning. For more information on members in your area, contact The International Association for Financial Planning, Two Concourse Parkway, Suite 800, Atlanta, GA 30328, (404) 395-1605. But as we advised with credit counselors, you should check references, consult the Better Business Bureau, and ask for the names of satisfied clients.

■ ■ ■

I have often said that one of the greatest secrets of my personal success has been to hire people who are smarter than I am. For every problem, there is a professional ready to help you. The other day I locked my keys in the car. I tried to solve the problem myself with a wire coat hanger, but after fifteen minutes of frustration and having scratched my car's paint, I called a locksmith. He came and within seconds had rescued me from my dilemma. Yes, it was costly, but I was successful in solving my problem because I was willing to pay the price.

Sometimes the cost of achieving your goals seems high. It takes faith to hire the right people. The good news is, there are people smarter than you who are willing to help you succeed! There are many people who are willing to be paid only if they perform well.

On your road to financial freedom, you will need help, whether it is with credit restructuring or investment planning. Mobilize your network. Hire smart people. Network your way to financial freedom!

Affirmation: *I have financial needs that I cannot solve alone. I won't make the mistake of thinking I don't need any help. Instead, I will seek out professionals who can best support me and assist me in my goals. After all, I am worth it!*

Step Nine: Capitalize On Your Experiences

"Success is never ending—failure is never final!"

A mountain road is seldom a straight path. It will twist, turn, curve, and wind around in order to get to its destination. Not infrequently, the road will seem to go for miles in the wrong direction before a turn starts it moving in the direction of its destination once more. But such twisting and turning is essential because on a mountain a straight road is not possible.

So it is with your financial goals and dreams. You will face setbacks, you will have switchbacks that may seem like you're no longer making progress. But take heart. The road is winding and curving, but it progresses toward its destination. You will make mistakes, wrong turns, and errors as you proceed on your path to financial freedom. But even these wrong turns can help you move forward if you learn from the experiences. Learn from your past. Review your previous mistakes. Stay focused on your goals. Then you will climb the mountain, moving up the ladder, rung by rung.

We have all made financial mistakes. The difference between success and failure is not whether you make mistakes, but whether you learn from them. Review your major mistakes and ask, "How can I avoid falling into the same financial trap again?" The three easiest places to make mistakes are borrowing too much for something you don't need just because the credit is available; borrowing money from friends or family members without a clear understanding of the financial responsibilities; and assuming that money left in a bank account will grow in value.

Lines of credit

When you have achieved some financial success, you will be offered lines of credit bigger than you have ever dreamed. Most of them will come in disguised form. You'll open your mailbox and there will be credit card applications offering low "teaser" introductory rates, promises of credit lines up to $100,000, and more. Do you ever wonder where these come from? A friend of ours works for a major bank that maintains databases containing more than 50 million names and credit histories. When you establish certain credit criteria— even if it is to properly consolidate your debts—a series of huge mainframe computers identifies your name and address and mails you those tempting lines of credit. Sometimes the application is even accompanied by a preprinted check that is made out to you, with instructions to cash the check immediately at the bank. However, when you read the small print, you'll discover that most of these banks charge interest rates of up to 21 percent for such cash advances and often assess a fee for cashing the check. Our advice is to throw these offers in the trash unopened. If you absolutely need a credit line, many credit card companies offer low annual rates below 10 percent. *Money* magazine and other national publications frequently publish the names and phone numbers of these banks.

If you are going to take out a line of credit, ask yourself what you plan to use it for. You should certainly not use credit lines for vacations or anything that does not hold its value. Using credit lines should be limited to items on which you will make a number of payments over an extended period of time, such as tuition, recurring medical costs, or home improvements. Of course, it is best to save for these ahead of time, so you do not have to borrow at all or can minimize the amount you borrow on your line of credit.

If you do take out a line of credit, avoid weak savings and loan institutions, which, if dissolved, can cancel all credit lines. And remember that a credit line is counted as a debt on your credit report, even if you have never drawn against it.

Home equity loans

If you are a homeowner who has consistently paid your mortgage in a timely fashion, you may find yourself being offered a line of credit in the form of a home equity loan. It is generally best to refuse these unless there is a definite need of a large sum of money that will increase in its long-term value, e.g., tuition or a home improvement. While a home equity loan is deductible on your taxes, the monthly fees can be quite high. If you must take out a home equity loan, be sure to be aware of the following:

- Look for teaser interest rates, which are a frequent lure for most home equity loans. Read the fine print. It is there that you will learn how much the interest rate can increase. I have seen fine print that allows increases of 3 percentage points in just three months or rates as high as 21 percent.

- Don't ever take out a bigger loan than you need. Instead, plan ahead for those large expenses you know are coming up and save accordingly.

- Look for a lender that offers a cap to the amount of increase on the interest rate.

If you take out a home equity loan or a second mortgage, you need to ask yourself if, when you sell your home in five or ten years, you will want to get out the equity or pay off the loan. If you borrow now, you will be reducing your equity.

Debts to family and friends

"The holy passion of friendship is so sweet and steady and loyal and enduring a nature that it will last through a whole lifetime, if not asked to lend money," said Mark Twain.

When you have problems repaying a loan from a financial institution, the situation can become nearly intolerable. But debts within a family are much trickier because failure to repay the loan with a friend or family member as scheduled affects many other important relationships. Many young couples have successfully borrowed money from parents for down payments on their first homes. Some financial planners believe the practice should be greater than it is. However, if you are considering borrowing or lending money with a family member, be sure to establish certain rules in writing so that each party knows what to expect. Even though it is thought that as many as 50 percent of all loans between family and friends eventually become gifts, you can avoid trouble by considering the following:

- List all details of the transaction in writing, including interest rates, terms and dates of payment, details of prepayment, and a provision in case of default.

- Discuss with the family member potential pitfalls of making the loan, including what would happen if the loan were defaulted.

- Ask yourself, "Is this loan more important than good family relationships?" Make sure you are aware of the potential consequences of lending or borrowing among family members.

If you are the one who is borrowing money from a family member, do everything in your power to do what you say you will do. Don't assume that the other person will forgive your failures. A good relationship with your friends and family members is worth more than money.

Why you should not leave your money in the bank

It is hard work to escape the snares of bad credit, organize your financial house to reflect your positive attitude, and save a nest egg that can begin to grow for you. With all that hard work, there is an incredible urge to just put the money in the bank and forget about it. While banks do provide a high degree of safety and reliability, they are not the place for you to accumulate wealth. You will not see your nest egg grow in a bank account.

Many people mistakenly believe that if they leave their money in a savings account, their money is free from risk. They forget that one of the greatest risks of all is losing your money to inflation, the cruelest tax of all. Inflation will eat away at your purchasing power. Money invested over the twenty years from 1973 to 1993 that earned 8.7 percent in certificates of deposit sounds good until you factor in a 3 percent tax rate and 6.3 percent inflation rate. After those two unavoidable elements, the result would be an average *loss* of 0.6 percent.

As you seek to accumulate wealth, you will need to address two basics risks: the risk of losing principal and the risk of inflation. While most people understand the first point, they fail to recognize the importance of the second. Inflation is always present. Sometimes it lies dormant for a while, but it is always waiting to raise its ugly head. And when it does, your buying power decreases. To fully achieve your financial goals, you must take some risks. But with proper education and counsel you can limit those risks.

■ ■ ■

Understandably, investing to outpace inflation can be a scary part of your financial adventure. It takes strength of mind and fortitude to move beyond the seemingly secure confines of your neighborhood bank. But with practice and patience, you will be glad you did.

Capitalize on your experiences. You will make mistakes, whether you borrow too much for something you don't need, let money borrowed from a friend or family member damage your relationship with that person, assume that money left in a bank account will grow in value, or some other mistake. Don't despair of having made the mistake. Learn from it and use the knowledge to continue on your road to financial freedom.

Affirmation: *I am on a winding road of successes and setbacks. I will not quit when I get afraid. I will forge ahead to understand my personal strengths and weaknesses. I will learn from my previous mistakes and try to avoid new ones. And when I do stumble, I will pick myself up and move ahead.*

Step Ten: Maximize Your Returns

"Make the most with what you have wherever you are!"

The parable of the talents told by Jesus as recorded in the Gospels is a compelling story of a rich man who gave money to three of his servants proportioned according to the ability of each. Two servants invested or traded the money given to them for a profit, but one servant immediately dug a hole and hid his money in the ground. After the master returned, each servant gave a report as to his dealings. When the master learned of the one servant who buried his money, he chastised the man, took away his money, and gave it to the man who had increased his money five-fold.

This story seems harsh to those who have a fear of investing, but this teaching of Jesus reminds us that there is no risk-free way to maximize your money. Even the foolish man who today wishes to hide his money in the ground or forget about it in a bank will lose his principal through inflation and taxation. Therefore, it is time to get the courage and the education to invest wisely and maximize your returns.

Books and books have been written detailing various options open to you as an investor. The purpose here is not to give an exhaustive list of investment possibilities, but to mention basic proven investment tools that will, with time and management, help you maximize returns.

Common stocks

The dizzying heights of the rising stock market in 1997 have made investing in stocks front page news. Individual investors from all over are suddenly joining in the action.

The stock market has traditionally been a good place to invest over the long term—meaning five-year, ten-year, or longer periods. Generally, the best way to invest in the stock market is with a diversified portfolio of stocks representing American industry and technology. This diversification is best achieved through mutual fund ownership. However, if you have the time and the inclination, researching individual stocks and joining a local investment club to share information and ideas can be a profitable and enjoyable undertaking. Since the stock market occasionally can be subject to sharp drops that can last, it is best to spread your investment money to cash and bonds as well. For example, some portfolio managers recommend 60 percent stocks, 20 percent bonds (with varying maturities) and 20 percent cash, although this varies with your age and financial circumstances. You can reduce your cash levels as you uncover good values.

Mutual funds

Today there are more mutual funds than there are stocks listed on the New York Stock Exchange. With such a large number of mutual funds available, you must be very discerning in your selection. There are mutual funds that specialize only in technology, in health care, in industrial materials, in home and building, and in natural resources. Choose a fund based on the current economic environment and your evaluation of various funds. Morningstar Mutual Fund tracking service rates the performance of more than 5,000 funds and ranks the mutual fund managers' performance in all investment climates. There are funds that charge a higher sales charge of up to 7 percent. And there are funds that are known as no-load funds which have no sales charge but have management fees. Read the prospectus of each mutual fund carefully before you invest and familiarize yourself with the mutual fund managers' track record both in strong and weak markets.

Bonds

As with mutual funds and stocks, there is a smorgasbord of choices in the bond arena. They range from series double E savings bonds, which can be purchased at your bank, to the newly issued inflation indexed bonds, which guarantee a certain rate of return above the government's annually announced inflation rate. Zero coupon bonds are popular in saving for a child's education because they are bought at a deep discount with a projected compounded rate that equals a specific amount at maturity. These are very volatile, but they can prove prudent for those with a small amount of money to invest and the time to let compound interest work in their favor. Most major brokerage houses, discount brokerage firms, and banks can provide information on U.S. Treasury bonds with a variety of maturities as well as other bonds.

Real estate

There can be little argument that over long periods of time home ownership has been both a personally enjoyable and a financially rewarding investment. Not only has it tended to outperform inflation rates, but most mortgage interest expense associated with home ownership has the tax benefit of being deductible on your federal income tax return. Most mortgages for home ownership also have introductory rates as well as lifetime caps to interest rates. Today's current low interest rates make for attractive low fixed-rate mortgages. Ten years ago, mortgage interest rates were 14 percent, having come down from 18 percent. Today they hover between 7.5 percent and 8.5 percent. Other benefits to real estate come from what experts would call capital appreciation on highly leveraged amounts of money; that is, your home's value can increase greatly though you started out with a small investment and a large mortgage. In addition, if you are adventurous, you can buy rental property.

Rental real estate can guarantee monthly income in addition to potential for capital appreciation.

The best way to maximize your returns begins with you. At the beginning of this chapter we said that the sentence "If it's going to be, it's up to me!" may be the most important lesson you can learn from this book. Recognize your responsibility. Maximize your results with the right attitude. If you can dream it, you can do it. Your success is an on-going process of reviewing the calendar against your accomplishments. Just because it is impossible today doesn't mean it will be impossible tomorrow.

When you set goals, put a time limit on them. As you seek to maximize your returns, determine how long you are willing to invest. Your investment plan is a day-by-day, week-by-week, month-by-month, year-by-year process of building a strong foundation. You will need to reinforce your goals against the inevitable sidetracks.

Proverbs 10:4 says, "He who deals with a slack hand becomes poor, but the hand of the diligent makes one rich." Success comes from deciding, daring, and *doing with diligence.*

As you climb this ladder of financial freedom, you are embarking on a journey of faith and determination. Financial freedom for you and your family is possible! I know you can do it!

Affirmation: *I have a dream for financial freedom. It is a good dream, a noble dream, a courageous dream. More than a dream, I have determination—tough determination. I am willing to work diligently to build my dream. I will put my faith in action through positive steps aimed to maximize my returns. I alone am there to see it through.*

Six

Ten Ways to Accomplish the Impossible—For Our Country

A debt-free America, one that is free from the shackles of a $5.4 trillion debt, is a big, bold, beautiful dream! The fulfillment of this dream will require the unrestrained commitment of courageous Americans wholeheartedly dedicated to producing creative solutions and willing to pay the price to carry them out. Whether we are talking about financial freedom for you and your family through elimination of debt or financial freedom for America through elimination of our country's crushing oppressive national debt, the path is the same: we must recognize our responsibility and make a commitment to fulfill a goal and a dream by paying the price and overcoming obstacles one at a time. The solution to both problems is possibility thinking.

We have asked economists, corporate leaders, senators, representatives, former presidents, relatives, waiters, secretaries, flight attendants, ministers, and countless others what they thought of our dream of a debt-free America. Almost everyone agreed that, yes, a debt-free America would be a wonderful idea, but almost everyone qualified that *yes.*

- Yes, if we do so without surrendering our position in the international marketplace.

- Yes, but not at the sacrifice of medical and social programs that insure the well-being of the underprivileged.

- Yes, but not at the expense of the collapse of our highways and infrastructures.

- Yes, but not at the price of eliminating research that can lead to incredible medical advances.

- Yes, when the nation can provide financial security out of its surplus rather than from its deficits financed by government notes and bonds.

- Yes, but how? How do you accomplish the impossible?

In the final analysis, all problems are essentially the same, whether they are intensely personal and apparently small, or whether they are urgent national problems of massive proportions. Problems are challenges to creative thinking. That's all they are. Problems are pressures to be more productive and inventive in our thinking. As we have said, "No person has a money problem, only an idea problem!"

I have seen small problems as well as enormous problems solved by playing the possibility thinking game. The technique is amazingly simple. Take a sheet of paper, write down the numbers one to ten, then force yourself to come up with ten solutions to what you have accepted in your mind as an unsolvable problem. Be mentally open to any wonderful, wild, eyebrow-raising, even preposterous solution to your problem that may come into your mind. You can expect to break out laughing more than once, for some of the wackiest ideas will quite understandably develop from what has now become your truly liberated imagination.

The point is that creativity happens in an environment of relaxation. The tranquil mind is receptive to genuinely creative ideas that form the seeds for real breakthroughs. Humor naturally relaxes a person, which sets the stage for creativity. Hence, what often times starts as a lark continues to become a spark.

So let's play the possibility thinking game and apply it to the problem of wiping out the federal debt. We shall offer ten possibilities that can contribute to paying off the debt. You can probably come up with ten better ideas, but let these suggestions stimulate you to believe that *paying off the debt is possible.* At least the possibility will emerge as potentially viable enough so that the goal should be taken seriously. If we play this game, by the time we finish these possibilities, the real issue will not be whether eliminating the national debt is possible, but why we should take it seriously and exercise leadership to go for it.

In 1985 we published a book, *The Power of Being Debt Free*, that called for many of the following suggestions. At the time, they seemed like a hopeful dream. But today these possibilities are much closer to reality. Had these ideas taken root and been implemented in 1985, America would not be in financial difficulty today. Over the past dozen years, the federal debt has nearly tripled. Today we have no choice but to buckle down and take back control of the government from the politicians. The tools we suggested in 1985 are still waiting to be used by elected officials.

Step One: Eliminate Government Waste and Cut Entitlement Spending

As Americans dedicated to paying off the national debt, let's first tackle perhaps the most obvious area, even if it is not the most critical one: government waste. Each year the government wastes billions of dollars, which contributes to growing deficits and larger debts. Therefore, the first possibility we propose to pay off our national debt is cutting back government waste.

We applaud the efforts made since 1995 to cut government waste by the Republican majority in the House. We also applaud similar efforts by President Clinton and Vice President Gore begun two years earlier with their plan to reinvent government. Such efforts are encouraging and are beginning to make a significant impact.

In our earlier book we shared an extraordinary interview with the now deceased J. Peter Grace. He had led, at the request of President Reagan, the Private Sector Survey on Cost Control, a commission that studied in detail ways the government could save money. It produced 2,478 cost-cutting and revenue-enhancing recommendations that could save, it said, $1.9 trillion per year by the year 2000. He met us at a restaurant in Newport Beach, California.

Mr. Grace pointed out that rampant waste in government was a major problem. "We found $424.4 billion in waste and inefficiencies that could be saved over the next three years," he said. "That's about $140 billion a year." According to Grace, the government not only wasted $140 billion a year, it also lacked critical information to collect the money owed to it. "The government is owed $850 billion," he said, "but that money has never been aged. The government doesn't know whether it is due, overdue, or when it is due at all. Eight hundred fifty billion dollars is three times the total taxes owed by all the taxpayers in America for three years!"

The commission found that more than six thousand dead persons were still receiving checks regularly from the government. "Between the years 1980 and 1982," Grace said, "there was $14.6 billion paid out in false payments by the Social Security Administration, including payments to dead people. The families who received some of this $14.6 billion apparently forgot that the people had died!"

Grace explained that fraud was a major problem in government, especially in the area of social programs. "The General Accounting Office said it had discovered more than $1 billion in food stamp fraud," he said. "We don't need the 963 social programs we have; we need only 10 or 20. There's a lot of fraud all through the government, and a lot of people in the bureaucracy are making their way of life by doling out money in both state and federal governments with the federal government picking up the tab."

Poor people were not getting the money allocated to them, according to Grace. His commission found that only thirty cents of each dollar allocated to help the poor actually reached them. The rest was lost or used in the administration of the programs. "Where did the money go?" Grace asked. "It's siphoned off to the bureaucracy. The needy people don't need that kind of help!"

In his book *Burning Money*, Grace told of a case of fraud that the commission uncovered:

> There was a contractor for the National Institute of Education who managed to do quite well at taxpayer expense. How? Let us count the ways: First, he held onto $71,000 he was supposed to pay to people attending a conference; then, he neglected to return another $25,000 in unused cash advances. Next, he used an undetermined amount of Institute money to support his other businesses. Afterward, he loaned over $100,000 of government money to friends and associates. Next, he overstated salaries by $23,000. Finally, this sterling citizen accepted, without comment, overpayments of $20,000 resulting from the Institute's inept accounting procedures.[1]

Inefficiency and poor management have led to some amusing but true stories reported in the media concerning the gov-

1. J. Peter Grace, *Burning Money* (New York: Macmillan, 1984), 3.

ernment's expenditure of our tax dollars. Mr. Grace asked us if we had heard the one about the $436 hammer that was identical to a $7 hammer in a local hardware store. In the same book, he gave the Defense Department's explanation.[2] Added to the basic $7 cost of the hammer were the following amounts:

- $41 to pay general overhead costs for the engineering involved in mapping out the hammer problem. This included twelve minutes in secretarial time preparing the hammer purchase order, twenty-six minutes of management time spent on the hammer purchase, and two hours and thirty-six minutes the engineers spent on determining the hammer's specifications.

- $93 for the eighteen minutes it took for "mechanical subassembly" of the hammer, four hours for engineers to map out the hammer assembly process, ninety minutes spent by managers overseeing the hammer manufacturing process, sixty minutes for a project engineer to ensure the hammer was properly assembled, fifty-four minutes spent by quality control engineers examining the hammer to ensure it did not have any defects, and seven hours and forty-eight minutes devoted to other support activities involved in assembling the hammer.

- $102 spent toward "manufacturing overhead."

- $37 for the sixty minutes the "spares repair department" spent gearing up for either repairing or finding parts should the hammer ever break.

2. Ibid, 88-89.

- $2 for "material handling overhead," representing the payroll costs for the people to wrap the hammer and send it out.

- $1 for wrapping paper and box.

This brought the subtotal of costs for the hammer to $283. This figure was increased by $90, representing the defense contractor's general administrative costs, and another $56 was added for a finder's fee for locating the specific hammer that fit the navy's needs. Another $7 was added as the "capital cost of money" for the hammer purchase.

A navy spokesman explained that large defense contractors are permitted to charge off general costs against all contracted items, and that in the case of relatively inexpensive items, these costs may appear disproportionately large. We have to agree; $436 for a $7 hammer does appear to be a "disproportionately large" price to pay.

Along with the $436 hammer, the military paid $511 for a 60-cent light bulb and $100 for an aircraft simulator part that actually cost only 5 cents at a hardware store. For the simulator part, that's a 200,000 percent markup!

Grace explained that such incidents were indicative of a philosophy that leads to overspending by billions of dollars year in and year out.

In cash management, budgeting improvement, and accounting measures, the government could save more than $30 billion in three years, according to Grace's calculations of twelve years ago, if it had managed by the following principles:

- Pay bills when they are due and not earlier unless there is sufficient beneficial reason to do so.

- Deposit checks immediately after receiving them.

- Keep as little money as possible in accounts that do not earn interest and as much as possible in interest-bearing accounts.

Grace's list of inefficiencies, waste, and mismanagement in government seemed endless. In almost every kind of agency, he said, some waste seemed apparent. There can be little doubt that government waste, mismanagement, and inefficiency greatly contribute to our rising national debt.

Reduce Entitlement Spending

Waste exists in most areas of government and entitlements are no exception. It is safe to say that virtually every entitlement program is administered less efficiently than it could be. However, the biggest problem associated with entitlements is not that they are wasteful or benefit only small special interest groups—although many certainly do—but that entitlements have become so pervasive in our society and that they tend to take on a life of their own. Once established, they become almost impossible to curtail. Entitlement programs were originally intended to provide assistance to needy citizens who could not sufficiently provide for themselves. But over the years entitlements have been expanded to include not only the poor and indigent, but also middle- and upper-income Americans. For instance, the federal government's primary housing entitlement, the home mortgage interest deduction, gives tens of billions of dollars in tax relief each year to homeowners, most of whom have annual household incomes of $50,000 or more. Many Americans who could afford to pay their own medical expenses cheerfully accept Medicare checks and then complain about the portion of medical costs they must pay themselves.

The fact that entitlements benefit such a wide spectrum of Americans is the primary reason politicians have such a difficult time bringing them under control. They fear making significant cuts in entitlements because doing so could cost them votes in the next election. While surveys show that a vast majority of Americans favor reductions in entitlement spending, few would support cutting programs that benefit them personally.

We, the citizens of this great country, must develop the self-discipline to pay our own way. We have become conditioned by years of government handouts to accept any financial benefits that may be offered. Too many of us say, "If others are getting money from the government, I want my share, too." We must find the wherewithal to say no to this mind-set—even if that means enduring some personal financial hardship—if we seriously want to help America solve its debt crisis.

When the 1997 budget agreement was developed, lawmakers took advantage of a huge revenue windfall caused by the burgeoning economy to increase spending for welfare, raise annual spending caps and allow $7 billion more spending in 1998 than otherwise would have been possible. They also agreed to provide $33 billion in additional spending for social programs—programs that likely will perpetuate themselves indefinitely and cause even more spending. The economic surge also enabled lawmakers to put off a major restructuring of Social Security, something that is desperately needed if the country's largest entitlement program is to provide benefits for the seventy-seven million baby boomers who will begin to retire in 2008. This group, born between 1945 and 1964, is more than 50 percent larger than the generation born between 1925 and 1944. By 2040 the number of senior citizens will be more than double what it is today and one in four Americans will be over the age of sixty-five. In April 1997, more than 43.7 million persons received Social Security benefits, and payments from Social Security trust funds amounted to $30 billion. With the projected shift in the age of our population—and fewer workers supporting each beneficiary— it is easy to see just how financially strapped the Social Security system will become unless it undergoes a major overhaul.

Through the years entitlements have benefited countless persons who otherwise might not have survived, physically or financially, without some form of government assistance. But since more than half of the federal budget is consumed by entitlements, it is only logical that many of the spending cuts needed to pay off the federal debt will have to come from this area. But we must be guided by compassion and common sense as we determine which programs should be cut back or eliminated. We should make every effort to retain well-run entitlement programs that do the most good for the greatest numbers of needy people. But we must also take a hard stand against those that are poorly run or primarily benefit special interest groups—even if we are members of that group!

Eliminating government waste is just one of the positive possibilities for paying off the federal debt, but it is the first step we must take to meet this challenge. It is also the most important step because it will not cost taxpayers anything.

Our government can learn a lot from an old parable. A wife came to her husband and said, "I would like to buy a new bed cover."

The husband answered, "What will you do with the old bed cover?"

The wife replied, "I will cut it up and make new pillow covers."

"What will you do with the old pillow covers?" he asked.

"I will use them for dust cloths," the wife answered.

"What will you do with the old dust cloths?" he questioned.

She answered, "I will tie them together and make a new mop."

He asked again, "What will you do with the old mop?"

"Oh," she said, "I will chop it up, mix it with ashes, and use it to stuff the holes in the outside of the house."

The husband was silent. Finally, he spoke. "All right. You can buy a new bed cover."

Step Two: Set Up a Legal Spending Limit through a Balanced Budget Amendment to the Constitution

The way Congress is currently set up resembles a situation in which 535 people have joint access to a major credit card—all with the same account number. Everyone can spend as much as he or she wants, but when the bill comes, each person will owe exactly 1/535th of the bill, regardless of how much he or she personally spent. Unlike your personal credit cards, there is no credit limit. There is no one telling Congress its purchase is denied because it is over its limit! Where is the incentive to limit spending?

Imagine standing at a retail counter, having selected all of your purchases. The clerk runs your credit card through for verification, and it is denied. Then you say to the clerk, "I'm going to take these things anyway" and walk toward the exit. How far do you think you would get? But Congress does just that. Congress can raise its spending limit and the ceilings on the debt, and then reach into the pockets of taxpayers or—worse yet—borrow the money and let it compound for our children and grandchildren to repay with interest. This is done year after year with little thought given to developing a viable plan to pay the money back!

Because the congressional credit card and checkbook are joint accounts, it is not hard to imagine what happens. Everyone tries to get more at everyone else's expense. After all, the bill is going to be divided among 535 representatives and their constituents.

We need to set binding limits on how much Congress can spend—immediately! Every other business and personal household has limitations on the amount of money it can spend. Now is the time to propose a *legal* limit to federal spending.

A constitutional amendment requiring the federal government to balance the budget every year would impose limits on the amount of money Congress could spend. Congress would not be allowed to raise the debt ceiling and borrow money to fund pet projects and please special interest groups. However, a balanced budget amendment could have a waiver provision for national emergencies, such as war or natural disaster.

In 1995 and 1997, constitutional amendments to balance the budget and limit federal taxes were drafted and came very close to passage in Congress. Both proposals failed in the Senate by just a few votes. There is still support among many of our elected officials for a constitutional amendment; however, passage of the 1997 balanced budget *agreement* could mean that lawmakers may not pursue a balanced budget *amendment* during the 105th Congress unless their constituents actively demand that they do so.

We supported a balanced budget amendment in 1985 in *The Power of Being Debt Free.* We were told at the time, "Forget it. It won't happen!" The naysayers cited every possible reason why it would fail: The amendment would have to be ratified; Congress would never give the majority approval; a constitutional convention would open up the Constitution to frivolous changes. There are always problems with every great idea. But a balanced budget amendment has now been seriously debated.

A major criticism of a constitutional convention is that extremists might want to question the Bill of Rights or make other proposals that would severely limit our freedoms or change the character of the Constitution as we know it today. To help ease the fear of a runaway constitutional convention open to any subject, a limit of one issue—the balanced budget amendment—should be imposed on the convention. A specific time frame, such as 120 days, could also be appointed for deliberation on this issue. Leadership requires recognizing problems before they become problems. We can't throw out a great idea because of problems that can be managed aggressively.

What once had seemed like an impossible idea has been on the brink of becoming part of our nation's Constitution. This issue is so serious and the needs are so pressing that no elected official should get in the way of its success by insisting on the support of his or her pet project.

Step Three: Impose an Across-the-Board Spending Freeze

A spending freeze would limit any *increase* in funds to existing programs for the next three to five years. Funding for existing programs would not be cut back; it simply would not be increased.

A flaw in the budgeting process needs to be corrected. Currently, each division of the government receives an increase in its next year's budget simply by spending its entire allocated budget for the current year. Although the percentage of increase varies, the principle still motivates federal employees to spend their entire budget. If they were to be frugal, however, their budget for the next year would be reduced. An across-the-board spending freeze would take away the incentive to spend the entire budget and should be coupled with an incentive plan to reward fiscal frugality. The economics of motivation would then take over.

Supporters of such a freeze say that if spending is held at current levels as the economy continues to grow, revenues will increase and deficits will therefore decline. When revenues catch up with the existing spending level, we will have a balanced budget. Over the past fifteen years, revenues and spending have both increased almost every year. Estimates are that if spending is held in check, it would take three to five years for the rise in revenues to eliminate the yearly deficit and balance the budget.

An across-the-board spending freeze would be an effective way of eliminating the deficit now without much hardship rather than paying for the cumulative deficits later at a greater cost. A balanced budget would be achieved without cuts in current services and without increases in taxes.

One of the first critical actions an emergency medical team takes in treating a hemorrhaging accident victim is to stop the bleeding. Congress needs to stop the bleeding of the red ink and deficits, and then it can focus its attention on healing America of its debt disease.

Step Four: Permit a Line-Item Veto

In 1996, Congress passed legislation enabling the president to veto individual items contained in larger spending bills. This line-item veto, however, was immediately challenged by a group of lawmakers as unconstitutional on the grounds that it interfered with the separation of powers between the government's legislative and executive branches. In late June 1997, the United States Supreme Court dismissed the lawsuit, ruling that since the president had not yet utilized the veto, the legislators had not been "injured" and therefore had no standing to file suit. While the Court's 7–2 ruling cleared the way for the president to use the line-item veto on future spending bills, opponents vowed that they would again file suit when the president actually does so. By sidestepping the fundamental issue of whether the line-item veto is constitutional, the Supreme Court has virtually guaranteed that this valuable presidential tool, which could help to eliminate government spending that is wasteful or favors special interest groups, will be bogged down in litigation for months, possibly years.

Why is a presidential line-item veto so important? Without a line-item veto, the president has only two options: He can allow an entire bill passed by both houses of Congress to become law or he can veto the entire bill. It is all or nothing. A line-item veto gives the president the power to veto or negate any portion of a bill while approving the balance of it. As we have seen so many times in the past, popular bills that were sure to be passed and approved by the president frequently contained many amendments unrelated to the main bill that ordinarily would not have passed on their own if presented as independent bills. Representatives and senators found that to be an attractive way to please special interest groups, and so it became a much-abused practice that led to government waste. The president and Congress alike, although they recognized the abuse and waste of the special attachments to major bills, were forced to approve them in order to pass the major bill itself.

For example, suppose the president supported a major bill calling for an increase in Medicare and Social Security payments to older people. But attached to the bill were twenty unrelated items calling for a variety of government subsidies such as low-interest loans to a major building contractor in one state or a subsidy of electric power for another state. While the president recognized that the majority of Americans would not benefit from subsidized electricity in one state or low-interest loans in another, without a line-item veto he would be powerless to do anything about the unrelated spending items if he wanted to pass the primary bill. President Clinton faced much this same dilemma in June 1997 when he was presented with a bill that would have provided emergency funds to flood victims in North Dakota. Attached to the bill were several controversial unrelated provisions—including, ironically, one aimed at preventing government shutdowns during budget stalemates—which the president did not want to sign. Had the line-item veto been in effect at the time (it was being challenged in the Supreme Court), the president would been able to strike the unrelated provisions from the bill and send the much-needed aid to North Dakota's flooding victims. Instead, the president refused to sign the proposal until the provisions were removed, which unfortunately delayed relief to citizens who desperately needed it but also saved millions of dollars by preventing passage of special-interest provisions.

We are hopeful that when the line-item veto comes before the Supreme Court again, our country's highest court will agree the measure is indeed constitutional, thus giving the president the power to delete from any spending bill those lines that are unfair to the majority of Americans.

Congress would, of course, be able to override a line-item veto with a two-thirds majority vote just as it can now override the veto of an entire bill.

The president is the only elected official voted into office by all Americans. Therefore he is not as susceptible to the pressure of powerful lobbies in individual states as are senators and representatives. Rather, the president is responsible to the majority of the people. A line-item veto would give the president the power to veto anything that he felt was wasteful government spending, and thereby help save each dollar to be put into effective use. When the line-item veto is finally upheld by the Supreme Court, we should start to see positive results immediately!

Step Five: Establish a Federal Debt Reduction Bank

We propose that the Congress of the United States establish and charter a Federal Debt Reduction Bank that has as its one objective to be the guardian of the financial future of unborn American citizens. How irresponsible would we be in our own personal debt expansion if we had no tough lending institution looking over our shoulders every time we wanted to borrow more money?

Our government has operated with virtually no fiscal restraint for more than two hundred years. The Federal Debt Reduction Bank of the United States would monitor and collect funds, make payments, and manage funds arising from all sources to pay off the debt. The monies received could not be used for anything else.

The Federal Debt Reduction Bank would actually assume the liabilities of the government and be responsible for paying off the debt. In turn it would hold title to the physical assets of the government in the name of the people. The collateral in the bank could be government lands and properties.

The Federal Debt Reduction Bank of the United States would have the responsibility of making sure that elected officials did not become reckless and irresponsible in their approval of budgets. The bank, along with a board of directors consisting of appointed persons, would ensure that politicians could not manipulate the budget to strengthen their chances of reelection at the expense of future generations.

The Federal Debt Reduction Bank would assume liabilities of the government debt under the following provisions:

1. The Congress of the United States could not incur any new debt without the bank's approval.

2. In emergency situations Congress could discuss with the Federal Debt Reduction Bank temporary loans with predetermined obligations to repay the principal over an agreed-upon period of time, not to exceed our own generation.

The Federal Debt Reduction Bank would assure us that specific funds allocated for the repayment of the debt would not be siphoned off to meet the needs of other programs but would be used solely to help reduce our $5.4 trillion debt obligation.

What would this do to the morale of our country if we knew we were on a program that would gradually, dollar by dollar, reduce our federal debt and at the same time promise a bright and prosperous future for our children and grandchildren?

Step Six: Increase Revenues through Changes in the Tax System

A wise member of the Crystal Cathedral board of directors, John Joseph, once said, "I am a success because I learned economics from my father."

"What was your father's profession?" I asked.

"He was a lawyer," John answered. When I looked puzzled, he continued, "My dad once told me, 'John, you can't succeed unless you understand basic economics. I'll give it to you in one simple sentence: When your outgo exceeds your income, it's the upstart of your downfall!' "

If we are to pay off the national debt, we must decrease outgo, increase income, or both. Therefore, possibility number six is that we should increase revenues so that the government has more money coming in.

In 1985, we issued a call for a radical change in the tax system and suggested that the flat tax or a variation of it might be most effective. The impact of such a change on the national debt, we predicted, would be dramatic through the increased productivity of the personal and corporate sectors. Back then, we felt like lone voices, repeating the wisdom of economists Milton Friedman and Arthur Laffer. Today we are no longer alone. In fact, many citizens and government officials have voiced support for a radical change in the tax system.

A change in the tax system must be dramatic enough to cause a significant underlying change in people's behavior.

Currently, people work diligently to avoid paying taxes. We should encourage people to work diligently—at their work.

One might think that in discussing changes to the tax system to reduce the national debt, we would be seeking ways to increase revenue by increasing taxes. However, the best way to increase revenues is to eliminate the entire existing federal income tax structure and impose a true flat tax. With a flat tax, people making $10,000 a year would pay the same percentage of their incomes as people making $100,000 a year. Various deductions that are currently available would be eliminated.

Opponents of the flat tax claim that it would shift the tax burden to the poor. But according to economist Milton Friedman, every class of society would benefit. The poor and middle classes would pay less taxes due to higher personal exemptions and lower rates. And although the rich would pay more taxes, they would actually be better off because money they now spend for nonproductive tax shelters could be freed up to be used in more productive ways.

But how would a flat tax actually yield as much or more revenue as the present system?

In *Tyranny of the Status Quo*, which he wrote with his wife, Rose, Friedman explains the process:

> The reason is that although the tax rates are steeply graduated on paper, the law is riddled with loopholes and special provisions so that the high rates become window dressing. The income tax does indeed "soak the rich," but that soaking does not yield much revenue to the government. It rather takes the form of inducing the rich to acquire costly tax shelters and rearrange their affairs in other ways that will minimize actual tax payments. There is a very large wedge between the cost to the taxpayer and the revenue to the government. The

> magnitude of that wedge was illustrated by the reduction in 1981 of the top rate on so-called unearned income from 70 percent to 50 percent. Despite an ensuing recession, the taxes actually paid at rates of 50 percent and above went up, not down as a result.[3]

Raising revenue by changing the tax structure to a flat tax is a viable option. But another possible way to increase revenue might be to actually lower taxes altogether. "Taxes are always a negative incentive," economist Arthur Laffer told us.

When the amount of taxes a person needs to pay is decreased, he will be encouraged to work harder and keep more. When taxes are lowered, people are motivated to earn as much as they possibly can. For instance, a person in the 40 percent tax bracket might have the opportunity to earn an additional $10,000 if he works longer hours or increases his sales. But after taxes, he keeps only $6,000. His motivation to earn that additional income is clearly less than it would be if he keeps $8,000.

If we increase motivation to work by lowering taxes, our country will see an increase in productivity. This increase in productivity will provide a broader base from which the government can collect revenues. The result is, for instance, that the government is better off with 20 percent of $200,000 ($40,000) than with 30 percent of $100,000 ($30,000).

Arthur Laffer is a strong proponent of this concept. He explained to us that the federal government is basically "taxing work output and employment, and subsidizing nonwork, leisure, and unemployment. It should come as no shock to anyone why we are getting so little work out of those who are employed and such nonwork and leisure from those who are not employed.

3. Milton and Rose Friedman, *Tyranny of the Status Quo* (New York: Harcourt, 1983-84), 65.

"If you want people to be fully and productively employed and wealthy, you should provide them the incentives to do so," says Laffer. If people can gain more from being unemployed and staying on government programs or from not reporting income, then they naturally will do so. In Laffer's opinion, the deficits exist largely because the tax system stifles incentives for people to work and pay fair and reasonable taxes.

"I dream of a debt-free society," concluded Dr. Laffer. "And the only way we can get there is through growth and prosperity."

Dr. Beurt SerVaas, trustee and fellow of the Hudson Institute and successful corporate leader, advised us that another change in the tax system that would benefit the debt is to reduce drastically taxes on capital gains. Dr. SerVaas said, "The media has confused capital gains tax reduction with a rich-versus-poor issue. In fact, many Americans have large portions of their personal assets in homes, farms, or small businesses that have appreciated over many years. If capital gains tax rates (which are in many cases higher than the individual's adjusted gross federal income taxes) were low enough to induce or encourage these Americans to sell, a large well of capital would be freed up, which in turn would stimulate the economy."

Dr. SerVaas suggested, for example, that assets held for one year could be taxed at 22 percent. If an asset were held for three years, it would be taxed lower at 18 percent, five years at 15 percent, and ten years at 10 percent. This would be a particular incentive to the elderly who have built and owned a family business over many years and who would be faced with a huge tax burden if the business were sold.

As we consider increasing revenues through changes in the tax system, we must keep three principles in mind. First, whether the change in taxes is to be a flat tax, a retail sales tax, or any other kind of tax, the rate must be low enough that people do not focus their energies on trying to avoid taxes through the use of tax shelters, unreported income, unreported cash transactions, barter trades, and other devices. Rather, taxpayers should feel good about paying their portion of taxes.

Second, taxpayers should feel good about the goods and services on which the government is spending their taxes. There must be a level of confidence that taxes are not being wasted. The best way to achieve this is through the immediate and appropriate spending cuts discussed earlier, coupled with our elected officials' demonstrating fiscal discipline through the appropriate stewardship of taxpayers' hard-earned dollars.

Third, the tax code should encourage savings, not punish savers by taxing the accumulated earnings on savings. This could be accomplished through expanded super IRAs, a USA (Unlimited Savings Allowance) tax savings account such as that backed by former Democratic Senator Sam Nunn and Republican Senator Pete Domenici, or savings for health care and education. Incentives need to be established to encourage savings. Already, many young people would prefer to opt out of Social Security and establish their own private secured pensions so that they will not be dependent on the government when they retire. Programs to encourage savings are essential in order to diminish the effects of our current welfare state.

We are not tax experts, and we make no claim as to what tax system is best. However, we do know that there needs to be a change made soon to encourage productivity. We propose that the experts, with the public's participation, hammer out the details and come up with the best plan—one that is fair and equitable to all sectors of society.

Imagine how much easier it would be if, when April 15 approaches, you pull out a one-page simplified tax form that reports your earnings and your appropriate share of taxes. You simply sign the return, stick it in your mailbox, and use the rest of the week to be productive in your work or your home or to enjoy your favorite hobby in the constitutionally described inalienable right of the pursuit of happiness.

Step Seven: Take Advantage of Lower Interest Rates

When we published *The Power of Being Debt Free* in 1985, we predicted that interest rates would fall dramatically. We pointed out that the real rate of return (which is the difference between what you earn on your money and what inflation eats away) historically had been two to three percentage points. In 1985, the real rate of return was 9 percent.

Using the historical norm of 2 to 3 percent for a real rate of return and the then-current inflation rate of around 3 percent, we predicted that interest rates could go as low as 6 percent for a thirty-year Treasury bond. In July 1997, interest on a thirty-year Treasury bond ranged from 6.55 to 6.85 percent.

All of this is a blessing in that it enables us to lower the interest rate on our $5.4 trillion debt. Now is the time for us to create a new debt instrument known as a Federal Debt Reduction Bond. It would have characteristics similar to Treasury bonds and notes, except that the money received from investors who buy these bonds could be used only to pay down the principal of the national debt. We believe that as the principal of the debt is reduced, interest rates could fall even farther because more money would be available. In fact, some economists believe that if we had no federal debt, our interest rates could be as low as 2 percent to 3 percent. Moreover, as the debt shrinks, the servicing costs of the debt would go down proportionately.

The interest rate on the Federal Debt Reduction Bonds should be lower than that on Treasury bills, but the interest on the bonds could be exempt from federal income tax or exempt from federal estate taxes so that wealthy individuals could pass them on to their children and grandchildren. This would encourage older Americans, who have a large concentration of the nation's wealth, to purchase Federal Debt Reduction Bonds to accomplish two things: (1) help reduce the national debt and (2) pass on part of their estate to their heirs tax free.

Step Eight: Sell or Lease Government Assets

Many government-owned properties could be sold or leased to the private sector with the income going to the Federal Debt Reduction Bank. Obviously, this sale or lease needs to be done in such a way as to avoid exploitation of the environment. Of course, there is potential for abuse or problems. But this just underscores a fundamental principle of possibility thinking: There is something wrong with every good idea. Don't reject an idea just because it has a problem with it. Every positive idea needs to be analyzed and dissected. Separate the negative part of the idea, isolate it, and eliminate it. Then release the positive element of the idea for its fullest potential.

Many government assets could be sold to raise large sums of money. Consider the current value of federal buildings. Does it make sense for the government, a nonprofit institution, to hold title to office buildings? As pastor of a church, I can tell you it does not pay for a nonprofit organization to hold title to apartment buildings or office buildings that have to compete with those built and operated by for-profit corporations. The simple reason is that for-profit corporations can deduct the interest on the mortgages as an expense as well as depreciate the value of the properties, all of which translates into a stronger bottom line after taxes for the corporation. Perhaps it would make better sense for the government to sell its office buildings to profit-making corporations in the private sector and then lease them back.

In addition, the government should consider leasing equipment and property it owns to the private sector. Services could also be leased. For years we have tried to get the Marine Band to perform at one of our church services, but we have been told repeatedly that the band is not allowed to play at a sectarian church service unless the president or vice president of the United States is in attendance. We would happily make a gift to the government if we could "rent" the band for certain religious functions. There was a time when California did not allow public school buildings to be rented for church purposes. And then the state had an urgent need for cash. Today public schools that used to stand empty on Sunday mornings are now rented to churches for their Sunday services. The citizens of the state benefit and the congregations benefit. It is a win-win situation.

Are there ships or other vessels that the government could charter to corporations and private groups for seminars at sea? Undoubtedly, many unused government properties, equipment, and services could be leased or sold to the private sector and generate billions of dollars to help pay off the national debt.

With the advent of new technologies, heretofore unrealized assets of the United States suddenly have become potential sources of huge amounts of revenue. In 1995, the government raised billions of dollars by auctioning off a small spectrum of the FCC-controlled bandwidth for use by personal digital assistance, a technological marvel that will allow people to communicate, send faxes, receive messages, and perform computer functions by hand-held, battery-operated devices. The future holds unlimited potential for the government to raise money in the constantly evolving field of technology.

Step Nine: Provide Tax Incentives and Solicit Voluntary Contributions

Each year billions of dollars are contributed to charity by people who are motivated to give money to a project or organization in which they believe. How much more could be raised by the people of this country if they knew that their gifts would help make America financially stable? Are we so jaded and so cynical that we do not believe that our fellow citizens would share the same sense of sacrifice and devotion as our founding fathers who pledged their lives, fortunes, and honor for their freedom?

We feel confident that this may be one of the most important steps that we have yet presented, for we believe that the American people are generous and grateful for the terrific opportunities they have inherited by being citizens of the United States. We propose that $20 billion a year could be raised from caring and concerned individuals. We believe that there are many people who would be willing to contribute money if they knew it was specifically earmarked for a fund that would help pay off the federal debt. The Federal Debt Reduction Bank could receive all monies in a special account so that people would know that their gifts were not being wasted by excessive government spending.

People love to contribute large amounts of money to great causes. In building the Crystal Cathedral, we received seven gifts of more than $1 million. We are convinced that there are hundreds, perhaps thousands, of persons in America who would be willing to make gifts of more than $1 million each toward paying off the national debt if they knew their money would be secured in a bank that guaranteed the management of our country's indebtedness.

It is not unrealistic to think that there are potential gifts to the federal government of $1 billion. And what about the millions of small gifts that could be raised? We believe this idea has countless possibilities. For a start, here are a few ways to implement this.

A Supertelethon

Imagine a live television program from Washington, D.C., hosted by our country's most respected politicians, the president, and famous entertainers that had as its objective to raise a certain amount of dollars to help repay the federal debt.

Every year, Jerry Lewis raises tens of millions of dollars in only twenty-four hours during a telethon for the Muscular Dystrophy Association. What a fantastic possibility a supertelethon would be to help pay off the national debt! It could last for a week, and private corporations could sponsor it to help pay for the air time, advertising, and production costs. All fifty states would have a role to play in raising funds. The personal involvement of hundreds of thousands of Americans would stimulate incredible momentum. It would help bring the country together to achieve a common goal. A financial upswing of confidence would also stimulate creativity and productivity to expand our national net worth to a degree that is unimaginable.

Even with possible large gifts in the million- and billion-dollar range, we know that most organizations continue to be supported by the millions of people who give smaller donations. The same is true with our federal government today. It is not the rich people who support our nation with taxes but average people who give their share. We know that millions of people would want to give their smaller gifts to the government to help repay the federal debt, and the results would be overwhelming.

Patriot Class Mail

The postal service could create a special patriot stamp that would cost 2 or 3 cents more than a regular stamp. The extra money would be deposited into the Federal Debt Reduction

Bank. Both the sender and the recipient would know that the person purchasing these special stamps was a part of a committed group of Americans dedicated to making our country financially secure for future generations.

The Walk of Freedom

More than ten thousand people proudly donated $500 each to have a window in the Crystal Cathedral dedicated to them or the person of their choice. We created an endowment fund to maintain the beauty of the gardens and grounds of the cathedral for generations to come through what we called the Walk of Faith. These are stepping stones around the property that have inscribed on them the name and favorite Bible verse of the donor who gave $2,000. The mile-long Walk of Faith not only served as a successful fundraising campaign, but it also has become a spiritual treat for everyone who visits the cathedral.

Perhaps the government could establish a Walk of Freedom to raise funds to help pay off the debt. For a $2,000 or a $500 gift, individuals would have their names, or the names of their loved ones, inscribed on plaques or stepping stones. These could adorn the Capitol gardens or the grounds around the monuments or other important sites in the city, and the millions of visitors in years to come would be inspired by them.

Incentives to give are very important in any fundraising campaign. The incentives the government could offer are endless.

Recognition on Currency and Stamps

In consideration of major contributions of several million dollars, donors could be recognized and thanked by their fellow citizens through an act of Congress so that the donor's face would appear on a determined number of $1, $5, $10, even $100 bills. The largest bill in circulation today is a $100 bill. With a minor change in regulations to allow persons still living to be depicted on our currency, wouldn't it be possible to print $200, $500, $1,000, and $10,000 bills in honor of the Americans who led us out of our national debt crisis?

Postage stamps could also be printed with the names and faces of donors who greatly contributed to our country's financial freedom. Private and public corporations and institutions could also be honored in this way for their fundraising efforts.

Highways and Parks

Thousands of highways that crisscross America's countryside are designated only by a number or letter. Why couldn't they bear the names of persons or institutions that made efforts to reduce the debt? Beautiful countryside parks could be named after the people who campaigned together to secure our nation's financial freedom.

Today between the Capitol Building and the Washington Monument spreads the magnificent Washington Mall. An inspiring Gallery of National Heroes could line this marvelous plaza, bearing in granite the slogans that are the foundation of our country along with the names of those persons who made major gifts to win an all-out war against the nation's greatest enemy, the federal debt. Let us give living Americans in the twentieth century the opportunity to make a contribution to their country that can be recognized for many years to come as a major factor in securing our freedom for future generations.

Irreversible Trusts

Charitable fundraisers have been successful when they take the long view. Colleges, universities, and nonprofit organizations do not always receive the gifts at the moment they are promised. Many gifts are given in the form of irreversible trusts.

By law, a person can give a sizable gift of property to a favorite charity. Then the person can continue to enjoy the capital earnings of that property or live in that property during his or her lifetime. The children can also be allowed to live in the property after the parents have died, and in some cases, even the children's children can benefit before the property is turned over to the charitable organization.

But in the meantime, the original donor can take a tax deduction of the value of the gift. For example, Mr. and Mrs. Smith live in a home valued at $500,000. They want to live in the house during their lifetimes. They also have a child and want the child to live there after they are gone. They turn the title of their house over to their favorite charity, whether it is a church, a university, or a hospital. Based on its current appraised value, the Smiths claim a sizable tax deduction that reduces their tax payments for the rest of their lives. And yet they and their child can live in the house. When the child dies, the charity can sell the house, probably at an appreciated price.

Many systems and procedures in operation today offer great incentives for people to give enormous as well as small gifts to charities. In a similar manner, an enormous amount of private capital in property and various equities could be left in wills and estates to the Federal Debt Reduction Bank of the United States with the understanding that the estate would be used to liquidate the federal debt.

Does this sound farfetched? Was it crazy for us to think that we could raise $20 million from voluntary gifts to pay for an all-glass cathedral? Yes! But big ideas do come to pass. And when a big idea holds the prospects of laying a firm foundation that can stand for hundreds of years, we have an idea that can capture people's imagination. We sincerely believe that tens of millions of people would be willing to give whatever they can to secure freedom for themselves, their children, their children's children, and many generations.

Every time we consider a new possibility, we give birth to a new set of problems. Every time we set a new goal, we generate new tensions. Every time we make a new commitment, we can expect to produce new conflicts. Every time we make a positive decision, we can expect to be involved in a new set of frustrations.

Possibility thinking challenges us to exceed our limits. This leads us to our tenth step.

Step Ten: Encourage Superproductivity by a Supernation

Our country has vast, untapped industrial and information-based potential in existing industries and the ability to create new ones. We have no idea how large we can grow in a healthy economy with low interest rates and virtually no inflation! Our tendency is to estimate our future accomplishments by our past achievements and that too frequently limits our thinking.

For more than two hundred years prior to 1996, the average increase in our nation's gross domestic product was about 2 percent per year. Many economists said that was the most we could do without triggering inflation. But for the past two years America's economy has been booming. By mid-1997, the economy was growing at a heady average rate of 4 percent, unemployment had fallen to its lowest level in nearly 25 years, and corporate profits were up 14 percent compared to 1996—yet consumer inflation, excluding food and energy, had dropped to an amazingly low annual rate of 2.4 percent.

What is the reason for this remarkable upswing in growth? According to *Business Week* magazine, America's corporations have revamped the way they do business through downsizing, outsourcing, and reengineering, and are making good use of rapidly improving information technology. In addition, worker output during the first quarter of 1997 rose at a rate of 2 percent, its fastest pace since the end of 1993.[4] This is superproductivity in action! In *The Power of Being Debt Free*, we said that we should challenge ourselves to increase the growth of America's GDP by 4 percent, 6 percent, or even 10 percent annually. We have achieved our first goal, so is it unthinkable that we could attain 10 percent growth or more?

As our economy expands at possibility-thinking growth rates approaching 10 percent, vast surpluses of capital will be available to pay off our national debt. Superproductivity by a supernation is the most beneficial way to pay down the debt. Everyone will benefit. It is the total fulfillment of the American dream—growth and prosperity for all! America is a superpower with superpeople who have superpotential for superproductivity. All we need is more superpossibility thinking!

There is no substitute in our electoral system for direct pressure on the House and Senate to be accountable to a concerned and aware public. You can write your elected officials. Share this book with ten people and ask them to get involved by writing their representative and senators. Let these elected officials know that you will vote for those who do the most to secure our economic future.

With additional pressure from the public, our elected officials can put aside their differences and devise a viable plan to eliminate federal deficits and repay our national debt. There is no substitute for a determined public, Congress, and administration

4. "How Long Can This Last?" *Business Week*, May 19, 1997, 1.

who will muster the political will to resolve this problem. All Americans must put aside self-interest for our national interest and our children's secure future.

We applaud the efforts that have recently been made by Congress to deal with the difficult choices that must be made to reduce deficits and pay off the debt. But there are more difficult choices ahead. Senators and representatives must not lose their resolve. And they should not assume that the American public will object to cutbacks. The backbone of the American public is stronger and straighter than they might believe.

■ ■ ■

What would a debt-free economy mean to you and me? What would it mean to your children and my children? A debt-free economy would affect every area of our lives, but let's look closely at the areas of housing and health care.

Lower interest rates would spur a boom in home ownership and home building. The lumber industry in the forests of Washington would go back to full employment. Glass factories in Ohio, carpet manufacturers in Georgia, and aluminum and steel factories in the East would all find orders pouring in. Factories for small appliances for kitchens and bathrooms would become superproductive. Companies that make boxes for shipping anything from light bulbs to plumbing fixtures would have "Help Wanted" signs hanging out front. The boom in our productivity would be fantastic! In addition, our children and grandchildren could dream of owning their own homes and paying them off in their lifetimes.

The money that is spent on nonproductive interest on the national debt could be used to fund more research into cancer, AIDS, muscular dystrophy, heart disease, diabetes, Alzheimer's disease, and a host of other ailments. Low-interest loans could be made to private sector companies and individuals to find treatments and cures. How many Louis Pasteurs and Jonas Salks are there with the minds, energy, and belief that they can find a cure for these life-threatening illnesses, but no research funds are available to them?

If America will decide to eliminate its national debt, it will have the financial power to provide homes for all its people, find cures for life-threatening illnesses, and build the economic foundation for the continuation of a strong and productive future. No longer will our country be laden with the emotional and financial burden of debt. Rather, it will be a country that knows the liberating power of being debt free!

Seven

A Declaration of Financial Independence

We arrived at the warehouse of Fleetwood Enterprises where we were to meet John Crean, founder and chief executive officer of America's leading manufacturer of motor homes, travel trailers, and manufactured housing. We knew he had built his company on a no-debt policy. Curious to learn more, we arranged to meet him for lunch.

John's wife, Donna, greeted us and took us down a hallway to a room where we could find her husband. We expected to see an office with a large desk. Instead, the room was a garage. Covered with sawdust, John stopped his work on a new, experimental recreational vehicle. Over a sandwich at a nearby coffee shop, he shared his story with us.

"I started in 1950 making venetian blinds for trailers. But at the time I couldn't get any credit. I had very little credit before I started the company, and what I did have was bad because I had been late on payments. So I was forced to operate on a cash basis. I bought parts for cash and I sold only for cash. I extended no credit. My sales policy was simply to sell a better quality product at a lower price. Well, I was into the business less than a year when my major competitor filed for bankruptcy. It turned out that when I started dealing on a cash basis, he ended up with all the bad credit accounts, all the deadbeats."

Shortly afterward, John began to manufacture travel trailers, and he was extended credit from many of his suppliers. "But I didn't like it," he said. "I kept careful records so as not to miss a payment." As business volume increased, so did his credit, and so did the credit he extended to his customers.

But then the recession of 1954 hit. Suddenly he could not collect his receivables, which meant he did not have cash for his payables. "I had $300,000 due to me in receivables, but I owed the same in payables," John recalled. "Since I couldn't pay my bills, there was a total shutdown in deliveries. When you are in debt, you depend on your customers to pay their bills so that you can pay yours. If you have too many unpaid receivables, you can't extend more credit and you can't sell your product. Then you are in trouble. It was a very discomforting situation."

Determined to work things out, John took out a $10,000 loan from the bank to pay his bills. But before his checks cleared, the bank nervously recalled its money. "I had prided myself on never having a check bounce," said John. "Now they all bounced. I decided then and there never to go in debt again, not even for one quarter. It was really a simple decision. Since then I have always bought and sold for cash."

Nine months later John was operating again on a no-debt policy. "Any economist will tell you that you can't do that in our economy and grow. All I can tell you is that it worked. In 1973, when the oil crisis hit America, the recreational vehicle industry was severely affected. Sales dropped off 75 percent. But because Fleetwood was a debt-free corporation, we survived while others didn't. When the crisis ended, there was a pent-up demand for RVs. We came out that year with the same profitability as every other year."

Today Fleetwood Enterprises' sales are estimated at more than $3 billion.

John's no-debt policy is not limited to his business. He and his wife have never had a mortgage and have always paid cash for their homes. "When you can't borrow money, and you see a goody you want, you know you can't have it unless you earn it. That gives you tremendous motivation to work. In 1951 my wife and I lived on a tight budget, but we always had a little left over. One day I saw this beautiful Jaguar XJ 120. Suddenly, I wanted every extra bit of work I could get just to make an extra buck to buy that car. I had it in less than eighteen months."

Run a capital-intensive business on a cash basis? It's impossible. Pay outright for your home and cars? It cannot be done. Live debt-free? We must be dreaming. But John Crean did it. His example shows that the impossible is possible, that the "can't-be" can be, that your dream is achievable.

Certainly John has demonstrated that you and your family can have financial freedom. When he started his business, he had a worse credit rating than you probably do now. And yet he built his business without debt. But John Crean also feels that a no-debt policy for the federal government is achievable and that it would greatly benefit the United States. He believes paying off the national debt begins with making a decision.

"I would like to see the leadership emerge that would make paying off the national debt as much a priority as winning World War II was. If everyone would produce more and tighten their belts, we could pay it off. It might hurt a bit, but if it were a national priority, it would be a pretty short-term thing. To get it done, it might take some pain and some long, hard work. But I'm willing to do it. I'll be the first to jump in!"

The Problem of Personal Debt

Is it possible that we do not fully understand the magnitude of personal debt in America? Consumer debt in America has more than tripled since 1980 and is currently estimated at more than $1.2 trillion. Mortgages represent another $4 trillion of debt. This means the average household in the United States is saddled with a debt load of nearly $40,000, and the amount is rising daily.

Advertising and the mass media have played a significant role in changing our national mind-set from pay-as-you-go to buy-now-pay-later. We have become a nation of spenders instead of a nation of savers. The proliferation of credit cards has also played a major role in changing Americans' attitudes about debt. Rather than saving to buy a desired item, millions of people now simply say "charge it"—with little regard to how much that item will cost in the long run. Instead, the only thing that many Americans want to know is how much it will cost per month. As more debt is accumulated and interest charges mount, the good life can rapidly become the bad life. Over the last three decades, revolving credit charges have skyrocketed from $2 billion to more than $300 billion, and the typical American family now spends more than one-fifth of its after-tax monthly income on credit card debt service.

Many Americans will incur so much debt beyond their ability to repay that they will lose to bankruptcy the lifestyle they borrowed so heavily to attain. This is why debt is the enemy of financial freedom. We urge you to take this warning seriously. If you are like the average American, you and your family have more debt than is good for your financial health. Your are facing a potential financial crisis and may not know it. We cannot urge you strongly enough to *get out of debt!*

The Problem of Our National Debt

Is it possible that we do not understand the enormity of our nation's debt? Annual deficits of more than $100 billion are staggering, but these represent just annual additions to the national debt, which in 1997 stands at $5.4 trillion. The interest payments on this debt are more than $300 billion a year. In 1997, we are paying $525,600 per minute simply to pay the interest on the debt! A $5.4 trillion debt amounts to $20,194 for every man, woman, and child in America.

But $20,194 of debt for each of us is not all there is! We are apparently not being told the whole truth about our nation's financial picture. With ingenious strokes of the accounting pen, our government has hidden much of our nation's debt. For example, unfunded Social Security payments, which amount to trillions of dollars, are not included in statements as part of our accumulated debt. Many quasi-government agencies are not included on the books of the federal government, but if those agencies failed, U.S. taxpayers would have to bail them out. For example, the Pension Benefits Guarantee Corporation, which insures corporate pension plans, was underfunded $71 billion in 1995. When Mexico faced its 1995 currency crisis, the U.S. dipped into its previously unpublicized Exchange Stabilization Fund to borrow $20 billion of taxpayers' money to lend to Mexico. High-risk loans and subsidies to special interest groups, which is called off-budget lending, are also not included in the outstanding debt. Estimates of our federal government's total debt, including these hidden debts, range as high as $20 trillion, depending on how conservative or liberal the interpretation might be.

A Declaration of Financial Independence

The power of being debt free is the power of financial independence. It is the power to promote peace, prosperity, and human pride worldwide. Of all people in history, Americans enjoy more freedom than any other citizens of any other country have ever known. How did we come to this freedom? It happened when people of vision, courage, and integrity signed the

Declaration of Independence and then formulated the Constitution with its Bill of Rights. These documents guarantee to every citizen in America the right to pursue peace, happiness, and the path of prosperity.

The truth is, each of us has the freedom to choose to become financially independent on a personal level. We can enjoy the feeling of being debt free and of knowing that we are giving that heritage to our children. With this freedom comes the ability to choose a variety of options in our personal lives. We also believe that a debt-free America is not only possible but essential for the future of our children. But we recognize that many people believe that paying off the national debt is impossible, unnecessary, or impractical.

I will never forget a visit I once had with a dear friend, the late Congressman Clyde Dole. When I asked him about repaying the federal debt, he said, "Why, we will never pay off the debt, Bob." As he saw my stunned and confused expression, he went on to explain, "You see, the federal government has no life span. As individuals, we all have a life span, and we have to think in terms of paying off our debts in our life spans. Otherwise our children will inherit a terrible liability, or we will face bankruptcy as old persons when we are incapable of earning more money. But our government expects to stay in business forever. So we never have to pay off the debt. All we do is pay the interest on the debt and keep refinancing it. We simply roll the debt over."

What America needs today are models of debt-free living. Commit yourself and your family to achieving financial freedom through elimination of your debt. But do it not just for your own personal benefit, but to demonstrate that debt-free living is possible. You and your family can be a model of what our federal government could do.

Let us repeat what we said at the beginning of this book. The road to financial freedom is not easy in the face of the seductive lure of easily borrowed money. For you and me that seduction is signing up for another credit card or buying an appliance on time. For the country that seduction is raising the debt limit. But additional debt only makes the shackles on our wrists and ankles tighter and the chains that bind us shorter. Increased debt restricts our freedom even more. Financial freedom is possible only through a change of attitude and habits. That is why our country needs thousands of individuals to demonstrate that debt-free living is possible and provides financial freedom and power.

Can we change our country's attitude toward debt? Of course we can. Until the 1960s it was fashionable to smoke cigarettes in the United States. You could smoke in restaurants, on airplanes, in offices, almost anywhere. Teachers smoked; doctors and nurses smoked to help keep them awake on their long shifts; learning to smoke was a way of demonstrating that you were growing up. There were a few health-conscious persons who warned about the dangers of smoking, but their warnings for the most part went ignored. From the perspective of today's awareness of the dangers of smoking, some of the advertising of forty years ago seems bizarre. Some advertising proclaimed the *health benefits* of smoking a certain brand. In another advertisement a young child urged his mother to smoke a cigarette before she disciplined him because it would calm her.

Over the next two decades, however, public opinion began to change. Mounting scientific evidence that linked cigarette smoking to lung cancer and heart disease led in 1971 to a ban of tobacco advertising on television. Many newspapers and magazines followed suit and refused to accept such advertising. For decades smoking had been synonymous with glamour in television and the movies, but its image evolved to one that was unattractive, even socially unacceptable. In the 1980s smoking was banned on virtually all airline flights in the U.S. More recently, as more Americans voiced their concerns about smoking's effects on health and air quality, smoking has been prohibited in almost all public buildings. Unlike the baby boom generation, which was bombarded with positive images of smoking, today's children and future generations will have the opportunity to lead longer and healthier lives. It is possible to change the country's attitude. It happened once over the last thirty years in regard to our personal physical health. It needs to happen in regard to our personal and national fiscal health.

We can solve our debt problems exactly the way we tackle and solve other problems: by getting down to the ABCs of mountain-moving, problem-solving, success-generating possibility thinking.

A—Attitude

Everything starts with an attitude. A negative attitude is certain to produce negative results. A positive attitude is certain to produce positive results. The financial crisis facing individuals and our nation demands that we examine our personal attitudes toward our own debt and toward the government's debt. Let's take the example of how our public attitude toward smoking has changed and change our attitude toward debt.

B—Belief

Impossible situations change permanently when a positive attitude evolves into belief. Negative thinkers say, "I've got to see it before I believe it." The error in that attitude is obvious. The truth is, we've got to believe it before we see it. In every situation we have the freedom to choose what dreams we will believe in. The history of individuals, institutions, and nations proves the thesis that what we achieve depends on what we choose to believe.

C—Commitment

Possibility thinking moves mountains when a positive attitude produces a positive belief that evolves into a concrete commitment. Again and again in sports, in politics, in war and peace, success does not necessarily go to the most talented or to the wealthiest, but to those who are the most committed. There are no great people. The difference between the so-called great persons and nations and those of lesser rank is a matter of commitment. Great people simply make commitments to greater goals. They dream nobler dreams. The greatest people in history are average people who have the commitment to tackle bigger problems than anyone else before them. The greatness of any generation will be molded and measured by the mountains it chooses to conquer.

D—Decisions

Possibility thinking works wonders because it is such a practical philosophy for creative decision making. In reality, problems are only decisions waiting to be made. Possibility thinkers are decisive leaders. Never do we surrender leadership to problems. We always let the positive, undeveloped possibilities call the shots. Never, then, do we let the problem-solving phase move into the decision-making phase. We make the right decisions simply because they are the right decisions, even if they appear to be impossible to carry out.

■ ■ ■

When is success really achieved? At the moment of triumph? At the moment of conquest? No. Success is achieved at the moment of *decision.* Decisions that become commitments hold within themselves seeds of success. Decisions become confident commitments that somehow the wheel will roll; the ship will float; the pistons will fire; the atom will split; human beings will fly faster than the speed of sound; we will walk on the moon!

You *can* succeed. Your children can know a family and a country that is financially free, but it will require an attitude and a commitment on your part. A positive attitude arising from a firm belief that you can succeed is essential, but action is also necessary. A careful decision that leads to a strong commitment is essential to accomplish your goal, no matter what the cost.

It is not too late if you act now to declare war on both your personal debt and the national debt. In the process, you will be declaring war on the poverty that may come to you if you have to declare bankruptcy or is certain to fall in catastrophic proportions upon our children if nothing is done today about the national debt.

One of my favorite parts of the Bible is the eleventh chapter of Hebrews (vv. 33-34, 37-38) because it tells of the wonderful ways that God worked in the lives of various Old Testament men and women. It tells of these people who "conquered kingdoms, administered justice, and gained what was promised; who shut the mouths of lions, quenched the fury of the flames, and escaped the edge of the sword; whose weakness was turned to strength; and who became powerful in battle and routed foreign armies." It does not say everything went easily: "They were stoned; they were sawed in two; they were put to death by the sword. They went about in sheepskins and goatskins, destitute, persecuted and mistreated—the world was not worthy of them." But the men and women described here all had faith in God: "And without faith it is impossible to please God, because anyone who comes to him must believe that he exists and that he rewards those who earnestly seek him."

Having confidence and faith in an all-powerful God and knowing that He loves you is the fundamental basis for a belief in yourself and your country.

The destructive cycle of lack of confidence in yourself and your government, which results in spending too much money, which generates a further lack of confidence, can be broken. Not only can we eliminate our own debt and the national debt, but we can regain our faith in ourselves, in our country, and in our God. That is mountain-moving, possibility-thinking faith.

Fifty years ago it was impossible to put a man on the moon, transplant a heart, or make a deaf person hear. The idea that you could live without debt might cause you fear of failure. The idea that we should actually try to pay off the national debt might strike fear of failure in the hearts of our president, elected officials, and top economists. Do we dare to run the risk of failure? Do we dare to stand up for what is right? Do we dare to disagree with the experts who say it cannot be done? Do we dare to share the responsibility for our economic condition? If you have the courage to believe in yourself and your country, you will find that financial freedom through debt-free living is possible.